I have watched my dad wrestle with God, Satan, pain, and himself. Still, he has done everything within his power to teach me (and my eight younger siblings) what it looks like to follow the voice of God. Dad's one message is this: The voice of God is to be followed at all costs, and there is no life outside of His presence. He has lived out this message, and he is the strongest man I know.

~ Kalyn Mullis, Age 24

Words cannot begin to describe how incredible my dad is; how genuine and how real he can be in the most tender way. I've watched him listen to God and pour his heart and soul into this book for years. I'm amazed by his strength, love, and passion for pursuing God with his whole heart.

~ Tessa Mullis, Age 20

In 2010, my father was awakened by the Lord and given a word that he has pondered for the past six years before publishing this book. Our family has been through some ups and downs, but it has been an incredible journey and an honor to stand by my father's side.

~ Josiah Mullis, Age 18

I have read many books over the past thirty years of following Jesus, but none were as transparent as *The Presence-Purposed Life.* Ken talks about his struggles and faith with a grace that has made a dramatic difference in my life and brought me to a new place of freedom. As a husband, father, and minister, I can relate to his story.

~ Kenn Kelly

I've known Ken for a long time, and if there's one thing I've learned about him, it's that he's consistent—his prophetic gift never wavers. Ken's insight has always been "out of the box" and challenging, as it commands change out of the old and into the new. I believe that Ken is a forerunner in the work God is doing in the world today and in generations to come.

~ Rob McKinnon

In *The Presence-Purposed Life*, Ken gives us manna from heaven and a light for the journey by making deep spiritual realities easy to understand while remaining theologically sound. Through his first-hand experiences, he shows us God's purpose for mankind—which is not so much duty, but "being" who God made us to be. Ken is like a John the Baptist crying out in the wilderness for such a time as this. Anyone who reads his work will surely desire to live a life that is more devoted to the Father.

~ Dr. Farris W. Cox, Pastor of World Harvest Church
(Dublin, GA) and Divine Design Ministries International

There are few Christian writers who can provide readers with a unique opportunity to understand real life, see into heavenly principles, and bring the meat of God's Word to the table. Ken's life, like yours and mine, has had many twists and turns but he has walked with the Lord through his experiences as a minister, musician, law enforcement officer, husband, and father. In *The Presence-Purposed Life*, Ken provides insight into who God is and who we are as a result.

~ Mark Taylor, Pastor of North Island Church (St. Simons, GA)

There aren't very many deputy sheriff's that turn into preachers, but then again, there aren't many men like Ken Mullis. I was close friends with his oldest daughter, Kalyn, during our high schools years. Though our lives have taken us down different paths, I have come to know Ken in recent years and have seen how God has marked his life with a message of hope for a confused world.

Though I spent a few years after high school avoiding my Charismatic roots, I can't seem to get away from them. Ken continually reminds me that no matter what I accomplish or how much I learn, the manifest presence of God must remain central to my life. At the end of our lives, God will not ask us to list our accomplishments or showcase how much of the Bible we have memorized; He will ask us if we ever learned to love one another as He first loved us. I have found that learning to love cannot happen apart from the presence of God, for it is there that God softens our hearts and makes us more like Him.

Ken has walked with me through one of the most difficult transitions of my life. He has left me countless voicemails offering prayer and encouragement, and has reminded me who I am on more than one occasion. He is a simple man from Georgia who carries the wisdom of a well-educated theologian. Grab a glass of sweet tea and sit down with your copy of *The Presence-Purposed Life*, which will make you feel as though Ken is sitting in the chair next to you, sharing God-stories.

~ Jared Stump, Founder of Living from the Heart Ministries
Author of Creation & Redemption: Finding Your Place
in a Fallen World

Senior Editor: Joy Henley
Contributing Editors: Monica Smith and Michelle Brooks
Cover Design: Alexis Benitez
Interior Design: Aubrey Hansen

Published in Houston, Texas, by Battle Ground Creative
First Edition

Battle Ground Creative is a faith-based publishing company with an emphasis on helping first–time authors find their voice. Named after an obscure city in Washington State, we currently operate offices in Houston, Texas and Harrisburg, Pennsylvania. For a complete title list and bulk order information, please visit:
www.battlegroundcreative.com

ISBN-10: 0-9908738-4-6
ISBN-13: 978-0-9908738-4-6
RELIGION / Christian Life / Spiritual Growth

Printed in the United States of America

DEDICATION

This book is dedicated to those who have experienced suffering, setbacks, rejection, hopelessness, humiliation, sickness, trauma, poverty, accusation, and disparity of life. To those who may have found themselves in a pit, outcast, crushed, bruised, and broken. Yet, they continue to notice the minuscule flickering wisp of a flame that still burns inside their hearts, keeping their eyes looking up to their eternal hope of glory.

This book is also for my wife, Christy, and our nine children, who have been on this journey with me, cheering me on as if they didn't notice the cost. I pray blessings over everyone who reads this book, that not only will you be blessed, but your whole household.

THE PRESENCE PURPOSED LIFE

A Journey to a Living Awareness of God

Ken Mullis

TABLE OF CONTENTS

FOREWORD

Years ago, at a low point in our lives and marriage, God showed me a vision while I was praying for Ken. I saw him caught in a web and being attacked by a larger-than-life spider. He was taken deep into the spider's lair to be devoured, but to my surprise he emerged from the spider's lair alive and free. I felt the Lord saying that although Ken had been attacked by the enemy, he would emerge from "no man's land" having seen things that few live to tell about.

Since that time, this vision has come to pass. Ken was attacked brutally by the enemy of his soul and lived not only to tell about it, but to reveal the character of a loving, grace-filled Heavenly Father who was waiting for him on the other side. The Presence-Purposed Life is Ken's account of this experience. It was painful to watch him endure the events he describes in this book, but there is so much joy in the love story that has ensued as he has discovered the Father heart of God and been transformed by His love.

I am proud to say that Ken and I have been married for twenty-eight years and we have nine children. (Yes, they are all ours!) We are close—very close. Ken's heartbeat is my heartbeat; his thoughts intermingle with my own. We are inseparable; we are one. Having spent so much of my life with him, I can attest to the reality that Ken Mullis is the real deal. He is a relentless pursuer of God's heart, a passionate worshiper, a minister to others, and a deeply loyal and loving husband, father, son, and human being. Forever pressing his ear to the Heavenly Father's heart and listening closely to all he hears, Ken always endeavors to be open and honest—even in his own pain. This vulnerability, quite frankly, is one of the qualities I find most irresistible about him, and I'm pretty sure God likes it as well. You can trust what Ken has written because you can trust his heart, just as I and each of our children do.

If you have ever felt down for the count, defeated, or disqualified, this book will breathe fresh hope into your heart. It will inspire you to continue running the race toward the high calling of Christ. No matter what you have done or what has been done to you, you can pursue God with everything you have and find peace and hope in His presence. Ken's message is that God's presence is the only thing that has the power to truly change us from the inside out. We must pursue this presence at all costs. It will transform our hearts, minds, and lives. This is truly a reformation completed by Love Himself. Ken wants people to know two things: God is not mad at them, and the Kingdom is not built by human hands, but by the power of the Spirit.

My prayer is that Ken's story will empower you to endure whatever painful process you may find yourself in, so that new life can be poured into your heart and you can be brought to a living awareness of God. You will then have your own story to encourage others.

It's time to believe again!

~ Christy Mullis
Wife to Ken and Mother of Kalyn Rose (24), Tessa Faith (20), Josiah Christian (18), Destiny Hope (15), Justice Michael (13), Jon Caleb (11), Malachi August (8), Mercy Grace (5) and Kori Bloom (1)

INTRODUCTION

This book is about a journey. Though it contains a lot of revelation I received from the Lord through a series of encounters, in the end, I believe God wants us to understand His relentless pursuit of our hearts. He, through the work of His own Son, has extended His extravagant grace toward us who call on His name. My hope is that, through these pages, a separation of who God is to us, rather than what we have often been led to believe about Him, will occur. I do not claim to have all the answers to every question; quite the contrary, but I do believe He is giving us keys to trust and follow Him at deeper levels personally, which are crucial in this hour.

God is calling us to a place of reformation—to a place of change that will challenge our thinking and renew our old wineskins, enabling us to contain the new wine of His Spirit. These things I have written are things I have learned, and am still learning, while on my own path as well. All of us who are called of God to be His children are on a life journey, and it is the journey that needs our attention. It is our awareness of God's presence that makes us aware of the path we are on. When we are aware of His presence, we will also be more aware of our journey. When we behold Him in His glory, we will also become more aware of our purpose and our spiritual surroundings.

Sometimes, using my own words to articulate what I've seen in the Spirit seems like such a disservice to that which I've seen. Yet, it is our uniqueness that each of us is given that paints the picture which cannot be orchestrated by man. So, this offering is my personal brushstroke on the vast canvas of life.

Jesus said, "I am the way the truth and the life" (John 14:6). What I believe He was really conveying to us is: He Himself, through His Spirit, is literally the path we are to follow. This enables us to receive the most hardcore realities that proceed from His mouth, presently. When we live in this place, we experience His life, in spite of the things that maybe swirling around us. When we learn to live in Him, in this way, our lives have become presence-purposed. Everything revolves around His very presence, and anyone can live there, especially you.

CHAPTER 1

The Encounters

ENCOUNTER NUMBER ONE

It was a Wednesday in the spring of 1997. We were struggling to make ends meet, and I was lying across my bed praying when I heard these words, *"Sell all you have and follow Me."* I jumped up and went to my wife, Christy, and told her what I thought I just heard. In typical Christy fashion, she said, "Let's do it!" In typical Ken fashion, I said, "Well, now, let's be sure!" Later that day, Fred McKinnon, a good friend of mine, called me and told me he was having a night of worship that Friday night, and he wanted us to be there. Fred was the worship leader at Christian Renewal Church on St. Simons Island. So, Friday comes, and we're on our way down to the island. I told Christy, "You know, if I knew God was really saying to sell what I have and follow Him, I would do it. But I'm concerned because my parents and your grandmother are getting older and I want them to get to spend time with their grandchildren. Nevertheless," I said, "I would go."

That night, at Fred's church, we had a wonderful time in worship. A couple of hours had passed, and I felt it was winding down when Fred said, "I still think God wants to do something else before we go." About that time, a lady in the back of the room stood up and prophetically said, *"So, you really want to sell all you have and follow me? Well, I've heard your 'yes,' and I am going to sanctify your 'yes,' but you are going to have to let the dead bury the dead!"* Uh-oh, that was us! Then another lady, one of the singers (I later found out she was the pastor's wife) walked up to me and said, "God's promises are yea and amen concerning you!" As you can imagine, the tears began to fall; I was awestruck.

The next day, I was watching T.D. Jakes on television, and he started preaching about David being anointed by Samuel to be king. While he was preaching this message, I began to feel like oil was being poured over my head. Wave after wave came over me, and I was doubled up with deep heaves and groanings pouring out of me. It went on and on. Even into the night, I would double over. I felt like I was getting a heavenly download too big to comprehend, and I was. I felt like I was being purged and filled at the same time.

The next day was Sunday, and I was still experiencing the episodes over and over into the night. Monday morning came, and I had to go to work at 6:00 a.m. with the sheriff's office, where I was a sergeant with the patrol division. I decided to stop by and eat breakfast at my mom and dad's. I started telling them about what was happening to me. I then started prophetically telling them what I believed we would be seeing in the last days. I saw stadiums filled with folks crying out to God. I saw

4

tremendous power on the spoken word, and many of them could not stand under it. God was touching the masses like I'd never seen before. I believed what was happening to me was going to happen on a massive scale. I prophesied these things for about forty-five minutes as my mother's tears bore witness to what was coming out of my mouth.

After this, I received a call that I was needed at the office. In my car, I heard, *"Prepare the way of the Lord, prepare the way of the Lord, prepare the way of the Lord!"* It was not an audible voice, but loud in my heart. I could not process what I was receiving because it was too much for my simple mind, but thank God He sows into our hearts. This event lasted well through Tuesday and began to wane, but I knew I had encountered a supernatural God.

After discussing these things with Christy, we put a for-sale-by-owner sign in our yard. Six months went by, and still no response. I just knew something was going to happen quickly, but it didn't. As Graham Cooke, a Christian writer, says, impartation can be an event—transformation is a process.

In January of 1999, I started reading *No Compromise*, the story of the late Keith Green. As I was drawn into the story, I began to sense the spirit of God the way I had during the weekend of impartation when I heard, *"Prepare the way of the Lord."* I felt something kindred when I read about Keith. I also read Christian evangelist Charles Finney's biography, and again I felt something kindred in my spirit. I was then introduced to the book *Why Revival Tarries* by Christian evangelist Leonard Ravenhill. I found myself doubled over, weeping and groaning with these fires of passion, as I had before.

In March of 1999, Christy and I were sitting in our living room. It felt as if something dropped into me, and I told Christy, "I believe I have the faith to step out and follow God." She said, "I do too!" We both felt like we just knew it was time. In two days, a man came and said, "Are you guys moving?" I told him that we were. He said, "I'm interested in your house," and he made us an offer for more than we had originally asked for a year and a half earlier! We also found out we could stay rent-free at a home Christy's parents owned in Eastman, Georgia, as we stepped out on this new endeavor. All of this happened in a week! I put in a two months' notice with the sheriff's office, and, in June 1999, we moved to Eastman, Georgia.

After we moved, Christy and I started playing in churches around the area. At that time, the way I ministered was usually playing and ministering the word in between songs. We saw some really neat things happen in some of those services and made some good friends. In one meeting, the presence of God entered in so heavily, two guys who didn't know each other stood up weeping and admitted to having homosexual relationships. Another guy confessed that he was having an affair. People were being set free.

After living in Eastman for a year, we started going to a church in a nearby town. We really enjoyed the worship, and there was a tremendous prophetic flow and the services were quite charismatic. Soon, I was playing on the worship team and meeting with leadership regularly.

While there, I attended a small ministry school. The classes were interesting and intense, and I tried to learn everything I could. As the days passed, I became friends with a couple that I went to ministry school with. One day, I was sharing with them about a desire I had to

6

record a live worship CD. I had been leading worship for years at this time and had been singing prophetically and spontaneously during worship since around 1990, and desired to record a live worship album in hopes of capturing this prophetic flow.

After sharing this with my new friends, they really got behind the idea, and in February 2002, we recorded two CDs: *I Will Run to You* and *No Alibis*. After we were finished with the editing, mixing, and mastering, everything looked like we were going to fly. Everything looked great on the surface. However, there was something underneath at work, something that was missing in my character, and this is where another story begins.

When pride comes, then comes dishonor; But with the humble is wisdom.

~ Proverbs 11:2

Pride goes before destruction, And a haughty spirit before stumbling.

~ Proverbs 16:18

PRIDE COMETH BEFORE A FALL

Before I tell you about the second encounter, I need to reveal some things that happened in my life between the two encounters. It's important that I do this so you'll fully understand the purpose for the second encounter.

While I was an officer, I was a Christian and believed I walked strong in my faith. I was leading worship at my church, and I took my job seriously. There are a lot of temptations in that line of work, but I seemed to easily resist them all. I worked out with weights, and when I was in my thirties, I could bench-press 450 pounds. I punched a heavy bag and practiced takedown maneuvers with other officers who were serious about their profession. I practiced at the firing range with various weapons. I took officer survival courses, building clearance, hostage negotiations—you name it. I was strong, and God was on my side—that was my mindset. I had overcome fights, bank robbers, burglars, and drug dealers. I felt like I was where God wanted me right up until the first encounter. I loved the time I spent as a deputy, and still have a strong affection for those who serve. I also loved the platform it gave me to witness to people in all kinds of situations.

Some really great things happened, but ultimately, the problem with this picture is that I had a sense of pride in my own strength and ability. I had a cockiness about me. I didn't fear men or situations that would have petrified me when I was younger. I loved being the strongest and the one that others would look to for help. I loved helping people. I loved high-speed chases, and was in many of them. I almost felt invincible. I was a very confident person in my own strength, and I believed that God was the reason for this strong resilience. I was all about living by faith, though much of that was presumption. So, when I had the impartation and the release into ministry, unfortunately, I took a lot of that attitude with me.

At our new church, when they told me they would be increasing my responsibilities, I said, "Don't worry about the mule; just load the wagon!" Can you see where this is going? "I won't fall, God is on my side, I'm the head and not the tail, blah, blah, blah, blah, blah, blah." After about a year and a half of stepping out into ministry, I was working hard to get our ministry off the ground. It was a little strenuous financially, but we were determined.

At our church, there were a lot of great people, and a lot of my time was spent with the worship team. I started having inappropriate feelings towards one of the singers. I could tell that she had the same feelings for me. I immediately told Christy and the senior leader of our church as soon as I knew I was in trouble. However, I was smitten by this attraction, and my ego was enjoying it. Thanks be to God that He kept me from a terrible mistake. I never touched this young lady, and we did what we had to do to stop it. However, a poison had been released into my soul that would almost undo me. I had developed serious soul-ties with this woman, and found myself unable to overcome it effectively in the current circumstances of proximity. The enemy had found something in me that he would use to try to destroy me. As much as my ego liked the situation, I had broken my trust in myself, and I felt powerless. I no longer felt strong, and I still had to see this woman every time I went to church. I tried to rebuke this evil that I could see at work in me, but a hook was embedded in my heart.

When I told the leadership what I was struggling with, they told me that, if I was going to be in ministry, I needed to grow up, that those who walk after the Spirit will not fulfill the lusts of the flesh. So, I tried to keep going, but felt imprisoned by the circumstances and what it was doing to my heart. I understood what Samson must have felt like when he lost his strength. For the first time in many years, I found myself in a situation where my strength seemed impotent. I was horrified.

Soon after these events, I stepped down from my position of ministry and we left the area, and moved back to Jesup, Georgia. I had already started working in a friend's timberland business, so I put everything I had into my work. I was so upset that these things had happened. The enemy began to have a field day with me. I was deeply depressed, hurt, offended, and just flat-out mad. I made the statement that I never wanted to be counted among anyone who called himself a minister again.

My business was booming, and I was making more money than I ever had in my life. During this season, I made more money in one commission than I had the last four years combined! In the natural, things were looking great. It seemed that everything I touched turned to gold. And in that area I felt great, but inside I was turning on myself. I still didn't feel free from the poison I felt in my heart. I was snakebit and becoming self-destructive.

I began to develop a rage inside which negatively added to my situation. It started to be directed at my family, and I was not about to let that happen, so I went to a doctor. He suggested I start taking an anti-depressant. So I did, and it helped me to not have the aggressive edge I was developing; however, I felt embarrassed about being on the medicine.

We started going to church at Providence Worship Center in Jesup. We had visited there before we moved back. In time, I started playing with the worship team, but I sure didn't feel like ministering. It was all I could do to go the meetings, and sometimes I didn't go. I had already had a mental breakdown. They knew I had been through a lot. I started feeling a little healthier day by day, but my battles were far from over.

Christy was pregnant, this time with twins. We were excited about the new arrivals, but three and a half months into the pregnancy, she miscarried. This was not the first unsuccessful pregnancy, but it still broke our hearts. My heart ached for Christy.

Business continued doing well, but by the end of 2006, I noticed a change and could see another storm coming: the economy was rapidly softening. I had my land ads in magazines. When things were going good, I would receive inquiries almost every day, sometimes several times a day. I traveled a lot. But I could see a rapid fluctuation coming, and when the housing market crashed, my business essentially no longer existed. That seems hard to believe, but that's the way it was. I had fully expected to have my home paid for in five years, but that was far from what happened next. In 2007, Christy and I had to file bankruptcy.

We ultimately lost our home, our vehicles, and all of our cash, trying to weather the storm. I not only lost everything I had, but also what others invested in what I said would work, and they suffered thousands of dollars in loss. The weight of this created an enormous amount of guilt and shame. I was experiencing total bankruptcy in every area of my life, not just finances. In June 2008, I lost my job. I was self-employed, but my services were contracted for a specific company. Because of the economy, they had to make adjustments, just like everyone else. I have been through a lot, but the loss of everything, on top of what I was already experiencing, seemed to crush me to powder.

I went from being deeply depressed to having suicidal thoughts. I had several breakdowns where I could not function. I would just lie in bed or ride out into the woods to one of the tracts of land we had in our inventory. I heard voices that were neither mine nor God's. I felt like God had turned His face from me because I was sure I had let Him down. At night, when it was time to go to sleep, I would lie down and fold my arms, like you might see in a casket, and would ask God to take me in my sleep. I now thank God for unanswered prayers!

I began having health problems. I hurt my shoulder one day while I was bench pressing. Another day, I was sitting up to get out of bed, and this bulge appeared on my stomach, just under my sternum. It reminded me of the movie, *Alien,* when the creature popped out of the carrier's stomach. I had a hernia—me, "Mr. Muscles and Fitness Guy." Then, I developed what I believe was gout. I had extreme pain and swelling in my knees, ankles, and toes. I could not even walk at times. I fell several times, scaring my children. One time, I almost fell through a plate glass window. I went through a period when I had double-vision. I had some upper back problems. I had abscessed teeth, one of which had to be pulled. I had arthritis in my joints. I had acid reflux. I had tinnitus; the ringing screamed in my ears. It seemed to be a perfect storm of issues that manifested all at once. I had no insurance and no money to get medical help. These conditions didn't last days—they lasted years.

I had two friends tell me, "You need to go to McDonald's and get a job flipping hamburgers!" What they did not know was that I could hardly walk across my bedroom to get to the bathroom. There was a season that I turned to alcohol for relief. I was destitute inside, and I had no hope.

I had minister friends telling me that I just needed to push through by continuing to minister, and if I did that, I would find breakthrough. Someone can be injured enough in his physical body to the point that he needs a trauma center followed by intensive care. You wouldn't go to the hospital and tell that guy, "You need to get up and get back to work. That's the answer!" Thankfully, we had some friends who had moved but whose house had not sold. We stayed there rent-free for a year and a half.

Through all these things, God kept me somehow. He identified to me the pride in which I had been walking. He delivered me from the need of antidepressants. He was still giving me revelation that I would write down. I just did not have a desire to share it often. Little by little, in spite of the contradictions, the chains began to fall off. Over time, I began to sense a small measure of freedom. I knew that I couldn't control my present circumstances, but I could control the intent of my attitude.

I began trying to find joy in every day. I knew I could be kind. I knew I could be gentle to my children, no matter what I was dealing with personally. I knew I could be kind to Christy. Christy says that I was pretty much always kind to her, though she knew I was broken inside. I was determined to glean as much as I could in this season. My family and friends would say that they just couldn't get over how gracefully we had walked through our difficulties. I thought inside that they might think differently if they knew all that had happened.

As we were entering into this season, before we left Eastman, Christy told me prophetically that she saw me going into "No Man's Land." She said it was a place men are not meant to see and live through, a place that most men never return from. But I would return from this place to encourage others and teach others what I saw in the enemy's camp. She said she saw me caught in a gigantic spider web, captured by the enemy and pulled deep into the depths of its lair. She is so sweet. God used the sweetest person I know to tell me that I was going to be sifted like wheat! It really didn't sound that bad when she said it, but every word she prophesied was fulfilled.

I had been sifted like wheat, and I believed at times that my life was over. In fact, part of that time I wished it was over. I felt like I had failed my wife, my family, both immediate and extended, my ministry, my business, and most of all, God. I was literally struggling to see how God could love me anymore. In time, I began to heal a little and get a little stronger, but what happened next changed my life forever.

ENCOUNTER NUMBER TWO

On June 1, 2010, about 3:00 a.m., I was awakened from my sleep and found my room full of the manifest presence of God. The feeling was very weighty, and I knew God wanted my full attention. I told Christy that the Lord was upon me, and I needed to leave and hear what He was saying. Many times, when I go to be alone with God, I drive out into the deep woods, where there is no traffic, so I can remove myself from all distractions.

As I was reaching the dirt road that entered the woods, I really felt in my spirit that this was the manifest presence of Jesus. I didn't see Him, but it was what He said that revealed Who was with me. I didn't hear Him audibly, but He was loud and clear, both in what He said and the experience of it. He spoke three things to me over a period of about an hour and a half. The first thing He said to me was, *"I'm not mad at you."* That's all He said at that moment, but when it was said, I not only heard the words—I experienced the words. I knew that I knew that I knew He was not mad at me. It wasn't just words. After He spoke that, I just felt like He was pouring this impartation of this aspect of Himself into my innermost being. It was far beyond my natural ability to comprehend, yet

I did understand in my spirit what He was doing. I could literally feel the chains of hurt and anguish falling off of me. I knew He was not seeing me the way I had been seeing myself. I wept and wept, but this time it wasn't from a breakdown of the past. This time it was relief from the poison that had festered in my soul for all those years that was pouring out, as His healing touch was pouring in.

This went on a long time, and I felt as if He was holding me. This feeling of His love for me never stopped through the entire experience. After this He said, *"Men get a glimpse of what I want to do in the earth, but then they try to build what they see with their hands."* After this was said, I felt His heart in His words again, like I did the first time He spoke. Great waves from His words were going in and upon me. I knew some impartation of what He spoke was being defined in my spirit. This went on for a while, concurrently with what I was experiencing from the first word. Finally, He said, *"Contend for My presence."* Then I felt the presence that we are to contend for. I knew this was a life message that was being imparted to me.

It always amazes me that one touch from His hand seems to trump all the years of studying His written word in a moment of time. And it appeared even what I had learned and experienced in the past seemed fulfilled. It's like all the mundane things I did now had great meaning and purpose. Even my weakness and failures seemed to have a sovereign purpose to them.

The residual effect from this encounter lasted for weeks. However, the Holy Spirit began a process of revelation which seemed nonstop. I seemed to see and understand things that I previously only saw dimly. The freedom I was experiencing was so wonderful. A real supernatural healing took place in my life. All the depression was gone, and I had an unreasonable optimism.

Within a week, I had a dream. In the dream, I was at a party. There were many people there, some I knew, some I didn't know. I looked across the room and I saw Bob Jones sitting in a chair. I had never met Bob Jones. I had seen Him on GOD TV, ministering at Morningstar Ministries with Rick Joyner. I knew he was a prophet, but that's all I knew about him. He was staring at me, as if he was looking into me. I walked across the room to where he was sitting. He said, 'Stay in His presence. Keep running to Him. The things in your life that still have a grip on you will fall away supernaturally as you keep going to Jesus. Don't even think about those things." Then he said, "I'm going to make myself available to you."

Bob Jones died not too long after this. I would love to have told him what happened in the dream. However, being that he is no longer with us, I believe he represents the prophetic ministry. What did happen was that I was heavily exposed to prophetic teachings and music through which God really spoke to me, as the transformation process had begun. Many times, I would turn on my CD player to listen to prophetic teaching by Graham Cooke, or some other prophetic person, I would hear about two words of the message, and be taken off into a revelatory daydream where I would just listen as the Holy Spirit would speak to me. Some might call it a trance. For some reason, the prophetic anointing on the CDs produced an environment where this process would happen. It reminds me of how music can be played and prophetic unction comes.

After this experience, I was infused with so much life. I began to participate at church with an inspired level that I hadn't been able to

16

access for years. I tried to be honest about where I had been, and I would speak what I was hearing. I understood that God chose me not for my strengths, but for my weaknesses.

Rick Joyner's book *The Call* describes a vision that he had. He wrote about receiving this glorious, shining armor. However, the armor itself was so bright and glorious that he would become enamored by it, and it blinded his vision to see wisdom. He was given these drab coverings to cover the armor so that his vision would return. It was a mantle of humility.

Paul said that he would boast in his weaknesses. I understand now that the revealing of our weaknesses is the mantle that covers the glorious gifts and callings in which we function. That is the mantle of humility. I'm not ashamed of it, but I sure can't be proud of it either. My weaknesses are the only things of myself in which I can boast without that boasting leading to pride. So, does the situation I'm in prove that I'm weak, or does it prove that I'm strong? It proves to me that, when I am weak, He is strong. Any greatness in me is the *free gift* that was given to me. Since it was given to me, I can't boast in myself, only in Jesus and Him crucified. I can take ownership, however, of who He says I am without boasting. I can boast in my weaknesses, and I can boast in Jesus to whom all power and glory are due!

Because of the things I have experienced and suffered, I bow my knees for those who have fallen or suffered the unreasonable attacks and stresses of life; that they may know the great grace extended to them; that they may know God is not mad at them; that, in fact, He chose them and loves them just as they are; that they may know God is the author and perfecter of their faith, and He's not through with them; that they have a future; that they may experience God Himself as the prize of life and hear His voice, and see His face; that they will sleep in the storm; and that their joy may be full. Amen.

In the next chapters of this book, I will share with you the revelation that came through this encounter I received from the Lord. When I started writing, I wrote for three months straight. I felt the Lord's hand on me profoundly during this period. This book is a part of that revelation that I feel is specifically targeted towards our individual journeys with the Lord.

CHAPTER 2

The Winds of Change

The winds of change are changing still. The term "winds of change," in its positive sense, has been used for years by politicians, songwriters, social activists, gurus, prophets, and preachers to announce and declare new ways of thinking or new methodologies beginning to surface. In the 1960s, Bob Dylan sang, "The answer my friend is blowing in the wind, the answer is blowing in the wind," and "The times they are a-changing," which spoke about social issues and the changes that were coming in that day. Bob Dylan was "preparing the way" for his generation and telling the world to get ready—it's coming!

The winds of change also occur in the industrial, technological, business, and artistic communities through invention, innovation, and creativity. Sometimes, change is met with fierce resistance through current establishments; in other words, the powers that be want to function in what has always been. When we use the word *breakthrough*, it's literal! Barriers have to be broken through. The sound barrier, racial barriers, social barriers, technological barriers, etc., are all areas where a measure of breakthrough has occurred. In the church, we must break the spiritual barriers we use that cap off and restrict the heart of God and the move of God toward us who believe. For example, we must annihilate the grace barriers, the love barriers, forgiveness barriers, offense barriers, or anything that restricts the Kingdom of God from being established in our lives.

THE SWORD OF THE SPIRIT BRINGS CHANGE

Historically, people have given their lives for such breakthroughs. Jesus is the greatest example as one who literally laid down His life for the greatest spiritual breakthrough of innovation and change known to men or angels. He defeated death, hell, and the grave, and established the new covenant. Others followed, like Paul, Peter, Stephen, and many more throughout church history who paid the ultimate price for their obedience to God, in word and deed. Even if a person was not martyred, they were often beaten, imprisoned, tortured, and verbally assaulted. Martin Luther King, Jr., is a more modern, yet classic, example. He had a dream that racial barriers would be broken. Once he saw the end result of his dream in his heart, nothing could stop him until he thrust the sword of the Spirit into the heart of racism.

God will so often, without anyone's permission, give a call or revelation to someone in a moment of time or a season. This revelation confounds and seemingly challenges everyone and every existing standard operating procedure. When God wants to break through religious tradition and the doctrines of men, He sends a messenger with a fire-shut-up-in-his-bones message, who plunges a sword into the heart of the very thing God wants overthrown in the hearts of men. Most often, it is the message He gives us that creates the very circumstances in our lives that shape and conform us to be a messenger. I sense the "winds of change" in the body of Christ. Some of which you may have heard before, and perhaps some you may not have heard or considered. One thing is for sure: the winds aren't coming—they are here. Change is here to be rejected or embraced.

I once heard Rick Joyner speak about a coming civil war in the church. I tried to imagine what that would look like. I tried to figure out what would be the issues that would cause such a war to happen, but through spending time with God, I can see those more clearly. However, I believe the war that was prophesied by Rick Joyner is here, and has already been started, and God Himself, through His Spirit, is delivering the first blow!

When we hear the term "civil war," we often automatically think about the War Between the States here in America. Now, you have heard my story, seen an individual divided against himself and the destruction it brings. I was a symbol of the church divided against herself, and I know how the enemy operated against me. The tactics he used to cause division within me did not win. Now I believe I know, at a greater level than I did before, the answer Himself, and his warfare against these devices. I am learning to use the weapons of his warfare. Love has lifted me up to higher ground, and now my journey is with the One who sees clearly, and He is the masterful genius in all that is good and just.

As much as we like to think that we have a revelation of His grace to us, God is uncovering, revealing, and releasing a greater measure than we have ever known. Instead of grace being seen only as a key to the Kingdom, it will be recognized as a foundational pillar of everything the Kingdom is built upon. We are saved *by grace* through *faith*. (Ephesians 2:8–9). Grace is not just unmerited favor, but also the power that enables us to follow Christ. It is the effectual power of the Gospel of Christ that is extended to us, the power of love. There are people who have a form of godliness but deny its power (2 Timothy 3:5). It's the way that seems right to a man that in the end leads to death (Proverbs 14:12).

THE TREE OF THE KNOWLEDGE OF GOOD AND EVIL AND THE TREE OF LIFE

I believe this civil war will be the war of the influence of two trees. These same two trees were in the Garden of Eden: the Tree of the Knowledge of Good and Evil and the Tree of Life. I don't mean that the two trees are going to be slinging their fruit and slapping each other with their branches! The war will be between those who feed from the forbidden Tree of the Knowledge of Good and Evil and those who eat His flesh and drink His blood, which is the doorway of the Tree of Life.

Most people have unknowingly fed from both in their local assemblies and even Christian television. Because there is a level of grace operational in most ministries, there still remains the leaven of the Pharisees and the leaven of Herod. I don't believe there is intentional malice on the part of most of these ministers at all. In fact, most are giving what they have, with all they have, to please God and accomplish

His will. I know this because I have done the same. It's just that the influence of the Tree of the Knowledge of Good and Evil distorts our vision to give truth or to receive it. Jesus, speaking to His disciples in Mark 8:15, says:

> *And He was giving orders to them, saying, "Watch out! Beware of the leaven of the Pharisees and the leaven of Herod."*

The leaven of the Pharisees is a hypocritical, religious system, while the leaven of Herod is a corrupt kingdom or political system. In Luke 12:1, Jesus says to His disciples, "Beware of the leaven of the Pharisees, which is hypocrisy." A little leaven leavens the whole lump (1 Corinthians 5:6). Hypocrisy is *not* when you proclaim to be a Christian, yet you have sin that is at work in your members (Romans 7:22–23). Hypocrisy is when you proclaim to be a Christian, and you pretend no sin exists in your life. When a Christian lives this contradiction, he places a burden on others that he himself cannot bear.

The apostle John wrote, "Any man that says he is without sin is a liar" (1 John 1:8, paraphrased). Grace, however, does allow us to reckon ourselves dead to sin, though the remnants of carnality may be at work in ourselves. When we are determined to follow Christ, saying we are dead to sin is not hypocritical—it's obedience. I will talk more about this later.

Now, if your heart is to do evil, then you are not living in an effective relationship with Jesus, because the fruits of that relationship will bear the fruits of the Spirit, which are all goodness, righteousness, and truth (Galatians 5:8–9). So, in your freedom, if you are determined to be a jerk, do not say you're following Jesus, because you are not. That would be hypocritical—you're choosing to walk in a contrary spirit other than that of Christ's, and you will become a slave to what you obey.

Paul said all things are lawful, but not all things are profitable (1 Corinthians 6:12). But Paul goes on to say that he will not be brought under the power of any of these things he is free to do. That's why Paul said we must work out our salvation with fear and trembling (Philippians 2:12). Let's face it, if we can't live in Jesus now, we cannot continually change. Grace enables us to change in spite of any contradictions that suggest otherwise. That's the good news! That is the Gospel. It's impossible to encounter Jesus and not change.

THE CONTAINER OF HIS GLORY

This truth will prove to be a major point of conflict. This will soon change, though, in many people and places, because mindsets and heart conditions will change, and life will prevail. We can no longer build in the way we have been building. The church is being restored, and the foundation is being upgraded to be the container of His glory that she was designed to be—the habitation of His presence. God is Love, and Love will win.

God is very intentional in what He does. He doesn't have to ask our permission when He wants to change or disrupt our theologies. When we walk in a place where we rely on the assumptions of what we think we know, more than what we hear Him saying, we set ourselves up to be resistant to change. That description actually defines how traditions and doctrines of men are established. Most all of us fall prey to assumption. It's the remnant of a fallen nature that tries to rise up again from time to time, and we have to guard against it. In Luke 12:49–52, Jesus says something profound that describes a certain intentionality He had about His purpose:

> *I have come to cast fire on the earth; and how I wish it were already kindled! But I have a baptism to undergo, and how distressed I am until it is accomplished! Do you suppose that I came to grant peace on earth? I tell you, no, but rather division; for from now on five members in one household will be divided, three against two, and two against three.*

He further confirms this in Matthew 10:34:

> *Do not think that I came to bring peace on the earth; I did not come to bring peace but a sword.*

So what happened to peace on earth and goodwill to men, right? Well, the battle is not with men themselves, but the demonic heart conditions and mindsets that hold men captive. *For our struggle is not against flesh and blood...* (Ephesians 6:12). The greatest enemy to religious traditions and doctrines of men would be anything that threatens to undo them. Jesus was perceived by the Pharisees and Sadducees as one who came to destroy everything they had built! Their perception was right. Jesus did come to destroy everything they had built. But their perception was rooted into the evil wisdom of this world. Their heart condition was wrong; therefore, they postured themselves against the very One who God sent to fulfill the law—the Lamb of God. He was the propitiation for our sins, the very Messiah, for whom they had been praying to come.

Based upon what they knew, through their perceptions, they *assumed* Jesus would come differently than He did. Therefore, they could not, and would not, recognize Him. The reason I said it was their heart condition that was wrong is because Jesus said, *"My sheep hear My voice"* (John 10:27). A right heart condition will always hear Jesus when He speaks. Obviously, they weren't hearing His voice in their hearts, or they would not have rejected Him.

This book will hopefully define in greater detail the ways I believe God is presently moving and what we can expect it to look like. One important key to victory that I believe the Lord would say about the way we approach this season is not to get bogged down by focusing on war. We will not be victorious by demonizing those who, in the natural, appear to be our enemies. The truth is, the greatest part of this victory will prove that some who are postured to look like our enemy will join us and become some of our greatest allies. The ways of our warfare are not carnal. Our focus must be on Jesus and staying in His presence. Only then will we see what we need to see concerning everything else.

WHERE THE TROUBLE STARTED

Since the fall, man's existence has always been determined and defined by the influence of one of two trees: the Tree of Life or the Tree of the Knowledge of Good and Evil. When Adam disobeyed God and ate from the Tree of the Knowledge of Good and Evil, he stepped from one reality of perception into another. Before the fall, he was plugged in, if you will, to God's heart. His perceptions were alive. He had eternal life, and he walked in that life. It was the very life of God breathed into him. When he deliberately disobeyed God by eating the forbidden fruit, his perceptions changed from God-consciousness to self-consciousness. Immediately, he perceived that it was "bad" to be naked and that it would

26

be "good" to make an apron out of leaves to cover up his nakedness. I find it interesting that he was more concerned about feeling naked and exposed than he was about the fact that he disobeyed God. But isn't that most often the case with all men? Before the fall, he had no consciousness of nakedness or sin of any kind. He wasn't thinking *this is good* and *this is bad*. Everything was life, and it was good according to the God-consciousness he lived in. Adam reduced his God-awareness of reality to a perception based on his own reasoning and the voice of his five senses, which were now corrupt because of the seed of disobedience that was now in his heart.

Adam was now enslaved to what he had given himself to (Romans 6:16). In a sense, he was grafted into the Tree of the Knowledge of Good and Evil and was destined to bear the fruit of that tree, including the loss of his eternal life on earth that would have sustained him. The punishment of sin is death. Since then, men have had the instinctive pull of the forbidden fruit. It is because of Adam's disobedience in eating from this tree that we have a fallen nature and experience death in the natural realm (Romans 5:12–14).

So here lies the mystery: was it the fruit of the Tree of the Knowledge of Good and Evil that was evil and brought death to them? Or, was it the fact that they had to deliberately disobey God to eat from it that caused death to come to them? Was it the fruit that distorted their perceptions, or the disobedience? Paul gives us the clue in Romans 5:19 (emphasis added):

> *For as by one man's disobedience many were made sinners, so also by one Man's obedience, many will be made righteous.*

God created the Garden of Eden and every tree in it. Scripture says that He saw everything that He created was good. So, the tree itself was not evil; it was the fact that they had to walk through the door of disobedience to eat of it. Therefore, disobedience opens the door to distorted perception. Now, any knowledge that came from that tree was distorted by their perception of it. Thank God that Jesus walked through the door of obedience and now He is the Way, the Truth, and the Life. We can now perceive the things of God because of the life of Christ, in whom we live. Jesus is the door we walk through to eat from the Tree of Life. Not according to our works, but according to *His* work of redemption—which is the free gift.

So, my food for spiritual sustenance cannot be a quest for the knowledge of good so that I can fix what's bad about myself and the world around me. If I could do that, Jesus would not have had to come. I've been made new, and a life-giving presence, by what Christ accomplished on the cross. Jesus said in John 4:34 that *His food was to do the will of Him who sent Him* (paraphrased). Now, from living and being in Christ, or abiding in the vine, I will obtain revelation knowledge from Christ that transforms me. Now I want to be obedient to Him. I was blind, but now I see!

THE KINGDOM OF GOD IS PRESENTLY AT HAND

When Jesus came on the scene, and when He was harsh in His speech, He was normally confronting the Pharisees, Sadducees, and scribes. Why would Jesus speak like that to the teachers and keepers of the law? Jesus was trying to get through to the Jews that the Kingdom of God was presently at hand. The Pharisees and Sadducees, as well as other Jews, resisted everything that He was doing and saying. In John 5:39–40, Jesus chides the Pharisees and Jews:

"You search the Scriptures because you think that in them you have eternal life; it is these that testify about Me; and you are unwilling to come to Me so that you may have life."

This is not the only time He rebukes them like this:

Jesus said to them, "If God were your Father, you would love Me, for I proceeded forth and have come from God, for I proceeded forth and have come from God, for I have not even come on My own initiative, but He sent Me. Why do you not understand what I am saying? It is because you cannot hear My word. You are of your father the devil, and you want to do the desires of your father. He was a murderer from the beginning, and does not stand in the truth because there is no truth in him. Whenever he speaks a lie, he speaks from his own nature, for he is a liar and the father of lies."

~ John 8:42–44

Do you think perhaps it was their vision and hearing that was distorted? Perhaps they were putting their faith in their perception or knowledge of the law—the very things that testified of Jesus—but refused to receive Him? This same kind of mindset still exists in the church today. If we search the Scriptures, pray, do good deeds, go to church, and preach, it still doesn't mean we are effectively coming to Jesus.

The Pharisees couldn't recognize Jesus, but the tax collectors could. The Sadducees couldn't recognize Jesus, but the prostitutes could. The "sinners" knew, if they could get to Jesus, then He would help them. The New Testament is full of stories where people pressed through to get to Jesus because they knew He was the only one who could help them. The woman with the issue of blood pressed through the crowd to get to Jesus. The centurion went to Jesus to obtain healing for his servant. Over and over the picture is created: get to Jesus, and you will receive help!

JUST GET TO JESUS

Getting to Jesus is the only thing that has ever helped, changed, or healed anyone. Our life's effort now is to live in Him, and help others get to Him. The chief priests and elders were more interested in asking Jesus who gave Him the authority to do the things He was doing. In others words, they were saying, "Who do you think you are, telling me anything?" "Who's your covering?" "Who's your Teacher?" "What network are you with?" "Are you Baptist?" "Are you Pentecostal?" Do you think a hurt and dying world cares? These kinds of questions came up in the church in Corinth—Are you of Paul? Are you of Apollos?— and caused such divisions among the church that Paul said in 1 Corinthians 3:1–4, when we talk like that, can we not see that we are carnal? These are the things of men, not the things of God. We need to know Jesus's voice when we hear it! Matthew 21:23–27 states:

> *When He entered the temple, the chief priests and the elders of the people confronted Him as He was teaching, and said, "By what authority are You doing these things, and who gave You this authority? Jesus said to them, "I will also ask you one thing, which if you tell Me, I will also tell you by what authority I do these things. The baptism of John was from what source, from heaven or from men?" And they began reasoning among themselves, saying, "If we say, 'From heaven,' He will say to us, 'Then why then did you not believe him?' But if we say, 'From men,' we fear the people; for they all regard John as a prophet." And answering Jesus, they*

said, "We do not know." He also said to them, "Neither will I tell you by what authority I do these things."

In Scripture, Jesus said that He, in and of Himself, could do nothing. He said that He only does what He sees the Father do and says what He hears the Father say (John 5:19). His desire was to follow and obey the One who sent Him. That was the authority from which Jesus said and did everything. The result of Jesus's life on the earth was that He never ate from the Tree of the Knowledge of Good and Evil, and He was the Tree of Life to all who would receive Him. God wants to manifest fruit from the Tree of Life through us, and all creation groans for the manifestation of the sons of God.

CHAPTER 3

Stretching Our Wineskins

Before I start talking about anything concerning new thought or revelation, I want to lay out a truth that has been laid out in Scripture. In Matthew 17:11, John the Baptist had already been beheaded, yet Jesus spoke of a future reference in time where He said, *"Elijah is coming and will restore all things."* For me, that says two things: Elijah is coming, and restoration must take place. What was it that Jesus was saying would need to be restored? All things! What does this mean? At this time, the early church had not begun and Jesus was already making reference to the fact that all things would have to be restored.

The disciples understood that He was referring to John the Baptist, and He was. But He also spoke of a future reference. What will this look like? Many leaders in the body of the church believe that it is an entire Elijah-type generation. I have no problem with that suggestion, but for the moment, I want to focus on restoration and what that looks like. Because when we talk about cutting-edge revelation, are we really talking about something new, or something uncovered that already existed and was lost through the ages?

Just because we've never seen something before does not mean it was not there in front of us all the time. Also, in 1 Peter, Scripture states that all things that pertain to life and Godliness have been deposited into us who believe. For this very reason, we bear witness to the truth of God. Have you ever heard something that just didn't sit right in your spirit? You may not have known how to articulate what you were feeling, but something was not witnessing with you. On the other side of the spectrum, however, we can also hear truth and reject it because of the years of conditioning from religious traditions and the doctrines of men. In Mark 7:13 and Matthew 15:8–9, Jesus speaks of tradition and doctrines of men, saying they bring the Word of God to no effect. He is talking about the living, active Word of God to us, through the Spirit of Truth and the truth of His word. Jesus is *The Word*. He was with God in the beginning (John 1:2) and is with us, who believe and go to Him— presently. So, just because something may seem foreign to us, we need to measure it by the word of God and the Spirit of Truth to make sure we are not rejecting *The Word* of the Lord to us.

Scripture says our minds are renewed by the washing of the water of the Word. We are transforming the inner man of our souls to live in harmony with the new creation we received upon being born again. The terms *renew* and *transform* speak of doing away with one type of thinking and being, and stepping into another reality of being. This is made possible by Jesus's work on the cross and the Spirit of Truth. If something we hear is the truth of God, and we find ourselves wrestling with what we have heard, don't worry. He is able to establish that truth we are wrestling with in our hearts. When this happens, our level of perception increases. We have to learn to understand and distinguish between what is not bearing witness with our spirits and what may just be troubling our souls, which could in fact be truth.

I personally have never had breakthrough revelation where I wasn't challenged in my core beliefs. There are biblical examples of this throughout Scripture. One of my favorite examples is when Peter fell into a trance in Acts 10:9–17:

> On the next day, as they were on their way and approaching the city, Peter went up on the housetop about the sixth hour to pray. But he became hungry and was desiring to eat; but while they were making preparations, he fell into a trance; and he saw the sky opened up, and an object like a great sheet coming down, lowered by four corners to the ground, and there were in it all kinds of four-footed animals and crawling creatures of the earth and birds of the air. A voice came to him, "Get up, Peter, kill and eat!" But Peter said, "By no means, Lord, for I have never eaten anything unholy and unclean." Again a voice came to him a second time, "What God has cleansed, no longer consider unholy." This happened three times, and immediately the object was taken up into the sky.
>
> Now while Peter was greatly perplexed in mind as to what the vision which he had seen might be, behold, the men who had been sent by Cornelius, having asked directions for Simon's house, appeared at the gate...

The focus of the portion of Scripture I want to illuminate is that the passage states, *Peter was greatly perplexed in mind as to what the vision which he had seen might be.* So God gave Peter a vision of a sheet filled with all types of animals that were unclean for the Jewish believers to eat. His initial reaction was, *"By no means, Lord,"* but he kept himself open to possibilities he had never seen before. He wrestled through the process until he saw the truth God wanted to reveal, which was not to call any man common or unclean. The reason we know this is because, right after the vision, Peter was summoned to go to Cornelius's home, and those there received the Holy Spirit. God knew that the Jews, during that time in their culture, would have nothing to do with Gentiles. They were viewed as unclean.

CALLING UNCLEAN WHAT GOD MAKES CLEAN

I thought like Peter once. I remember, years ago, the first time I started hearing about five-fold ministry as described in Ephesians 4:11–16, which is speaking of today's existence of apostles, prophets, evangelists, pastors, and teachers. I have to say that I was slightly shocked and skeptical of what I was hearing, because I had been conditioned to reject the idea that this could still exist. But God prepares the way for each dispensation that He wants to release in the earth in His proper time. I am now at peace about five-fold ministry. But I don't want five-fold ministry to be the focus, it's about calling unclean or bad what God has made clean or good.

For all of his life, Peter had been conditioned to believe that the Gentiles were unclean. When God gave him the vision of the sheet with all the animals and God said kill and eat, Peter had the assurance that Christianity was for all men. It was at that point that he knew Christ was for *all* men. Then he went to Cornelius's house and saw the Gentiles there get filled with the Holy Spirit. He was growing up in the things of God because he embraced the vision the Lord put before him.

John the Baptist prepared the way for the coming of Jesus and the Kingdom of Heaven. God always sends someone to manifest His very presence in such a way that He is able to instruct, pluck up obstacles, and impart revelation and vision. Preparing the way could also be likened to stretching the wineskins to be able to contain the new wine, as in Matthew 9:16–17.

> *"But no one puts a patch of unshrunk cloth on an old garment; for the patch pulls away from the garment, and a worse tear results. Nor do people put new wine into old wineskins; otherwise the wineskins burst, and the wine pours out, and the wineskins are ruined; but they put new wine into fresh wineskins, and both are preserved."*

GOD IS STRETCHING US

When God is stretching us and making us pliable, He may allow circumstances to occur that our wrong theology cannot fix. Or He may do with us, perhaps, what He did with Peter, and drop a sheet down from Heaven, showing us something that may appear offensive to us at first. That is why we must know our Lord's voice. Peter knew it well enough that, even though what he saw offended him, he knew the Lord was trying to convey a matter to His heart.

During the time we were going through so much, as I described earlier, my wife Christy had been going to some meetings in a town nearby. She would come home and tell me how wonderful the meetings were and how wonderful the teaching was. I reluctantly decided to go to the next meeting. I got there and the worship was good. They wrapped up that portion of the service and introduced the speaker, and as soon as he began to speak, laughter started breaking out. Everyone was laughing with hysteria. There was no teaching, and they immediately formed a fire tunnel.

For any of you that don't know what a fire tunnel is, it's when two lines are formed, similar to a gauntlet. One by one people walk through the line as each one lays hands on those passing through. The purpose of this is for impartation and blessing. People were falling and laughing and the longer it was happening, the angrier I was getting inside. I did not feel anything of what was obviously happening. I felt like I was either a stick in the mud, or they were all crazy. I was in need of help during that time. Could it be that I was so offended by the way the Lord appeared to move that I rejected His method to bring healing into my life? Was God trying to stretch me and make me pliable for "new wine"?

Mary, the mother of Jesus, had the opportunity to scratch her head in wonder. God sent an angel to proclaim what He was going to do through her. He told her the Holy Spirit would overshadow her and she would become pregnant with our Savior, and her response was, *"May it be done to me according to your word"* (Luke 1:38). God always prepares us if we have ears to hear.

I heard the term "wind of change" a few years ago from a pastor friend of mine. He had a dream and called for my input. In the dream, he saw a tornado headed straight towards him. His first reaction to what he saw was to rebuke this tornado that looked as if it would devastate everything in its path. However, after pondering all the elements in the dream, he realized that he was rebuking the very wind God was sending into the body of Christ for the purpose of change. The last thing he heard before he awakened was "wind of change." Another friend of mine who has received some training in dream interpretation said that a tornado represents a force that changes the landscape. Could God be initiating change to our existing spiritual landscape? The dream certainly reflected what God wanted to do in the earth concerning His church and some of the fears that would arise in us when it took place.

Either that day or the next, my pastor read a prophetic word where Bob Jones saw an angel named *Wind of Change* being released to minister in cooperation with a third wave of revival that would spread and not end. This is exciting to ponder. What I feel led to point out is not so much the proclamations of the change, but what it might look like, what it seems like to us, who have been holding onto religious tradition and the doctrines of men.

I believe my friend's initial reaction to the dream reflects the heart of many in the body of Christ and where we are as believers. His first reaction to the "Wind of Change" was to rebuke it as an evil, destructive force that is on a collision course with the Church as we know it. What would lead us to rebuke something God is saying or doing? I remember a quote by Dr. Kenneth Hagin, and I paraphrase, "Whatever you're not up on you tend to be down on." That says a lot. We as humans do not like something unexplainable that can't be labeled or put in a box. We like rules and formulas to live by. We love to try to make everything fit according to our perceptions of what we believe is acceptable. We don't like things that look different or tend to change the way we may appear to our Christian peers and society, which is more deeply rooted in the fear of man than of God.

Art is a good example of diverse thought and expression. Art is as unique as the artist who releases his or her art, whether it's music, painting, or sculpting. This uniqueness from a pure heart is the vast beauty and heart of God being released in the earth. In the United States alone, there are many cultures that coexist in one country. When a culture has embraced God and His word, it will reflect His nature through the diversity that comes within the culture.

GOD WANTED THEM JUST AS THEY WERE

If a rock band gets saved and comes out from where they were, they still have to bring themselves with them! That doesn't mean they stay in a sinful condition, but if they like the sound of rock music before they are born again, they will probably like that sound after they are born again. Hopefully, they will transform from wanting to *be* worshipped to *worshipping and exalting their Savior with their lives*, and that doesn't necessarily mean they are to start playing in a church service. God is able to keep them positioned where He found them if He chooses. Yet, if they got involved with a local church and started writing songs for praise and worship, what do you think it is going to sound like? Probably not the Gaither Vocal Band, nor should it! That expression of God already exists. Why would God purchase a rock band at such a great price? Because He specifically wanted them just as they were at that moment. Don't get me wrong; the driving motivational force behind some music can come from demonic origins, but a genre in itself is not evil. It is merely a unique way of artistic expression.

Some music can be sensual, but that doesn't necessarily make it evil. For example, if you are married, you have a sensual relationship with your wife. When you are together, you may enjoy sensual music for the atmosphere it creates, and it will be totally okay with God. However, if you are with your neighbor's wife, you should not be listening to sensual music with her, because you don't have a sensual relationship with her. There is power in certain types of music that can create an unholy atmosphere which would not be appropriate in all relationships. Genres of music act as a vehicle that can lead to life or death, dependent on the spirit of intention of the song, or how you hear it. Any genre can be used to produce life or death, but how you hear can also produce life or death (Luke 8:18).

Now, the challenge for the church is where will we let the rockers, rappers, and other so-called un-Christian types fit in with the rest of us? I am a musician. I've been playing in churches for a long time, and early on I slightly departed from the kind of music that was dear to me, for the purpose of fitting in. For me, that led to frustration. I have now abandoned that mindset because God loves uniqueness and diversity. I can't tell you how many times that, when people heard me play, they wanted me to come play just for their youth, but not for the main service, because I was contemporary. Honestly, they are just rejecting what they cannot embrace, subconsciously thinking it's not clean enough for an adult service.

I love playing for youth, but I'm now in my fifties, and I still like the style of music I've always played. Most people my age grew up listening to all types of music, yet it seems strange to some of them that that kind of music could be played in a church service. It's funny to me what we see as "acceptable church music." Not only that, but why would we want our youth hearing something we would be afraid of allowing before our entire congregations?

Do adult Christians only like hymns or conservative worship choruses? To be honest, I believe that some Christians would be far more comfortable if I were playing in a bar than in church, but why is that? What I'm saying is not intended to sound irreverent, and holiness should never be compromised. But are we calling something unholy that God made holy? Remember Peter, when the sheet came down before him in the vision and the Lord told Peter to kill and eat?

Anything we see or hear that makes us uncomfortable may seem as uncontrollable as a tornado to us. Our fears and doubts may overtake us, and we may feel that we would be doing God a service to stop it. Jesus remarked on this very thing in John 16:2, *"They will make you outcasts from the synagogue, but an hour is coming for everyone who kills you to think that he is offering service to God."*

We think we have to keep the house of God looking a certain way or we will lose control. Does God really depend on you to steady His ark? Where were you, o man, when the foundations of the earth were laid (Job 38:4)? We think God would not do something a certain way, only because we wouldn't do it that way, which reveals a little bit about who we really serve—ourselves! When we think that way, what we are doing is reducing God's infinite ability to our limited perception. That sounds like the wrong tree to me. If we feel that way, we really think way too highly of ourselves. We would rather spiritually clone ourselves than to experience diversity and change from others.

God wants this diverse spectrum of who He is, through our uniqueness, to reflect His multifaceted vastness. He may come to us in a number of ways that we can't imagine, and it will be our responsibility to know His voice. When He comes in His uniqueness, there are definitive attributes that will be experienced. There will be fruits of the Spirit: power, love, grace, freedom, and great blessing, to those who have ears to hear. But just as sure as there are those good things, there will be persecution, division, and other works of the flesh that will manifest around us, as the result of it. Everywhere Jesus went, devils would manifest, and as they did, He would undo their works.

TREASURE IN EARTHEN VESSELS

I have heard it said that transformation is a process, not an event. I believe that to be true. So often we hope for a quick way past our issues and problems, and sometimes it is rapid. People travel to Christian conferences and meetings in hopes of freedom from burdens and struggles, and God does want to bring healing, encouragement, revelation, and hope to us. I love anointed services, and as Bill Johnson of Bethel Church in Redding, California, says, "Wise men are still willing to travel for the anointing." But the process of transformation from the "babe in Christ" to a "Father in the Spirit" usually takes years of following Christ. I do want to say, however, that where we are in that process does not limit the miraculous works of God towards us, even while we are in the process of change. Remember, Peter walked on water, and he was not even born again or filled with the Spirit when he did it.

God's blessings toward us are not contingent on our perfected Christian walk, but on the perfected work of Jesus's death, burial, and resurrection! That takes away our excuses, doesn't it? What I'm relating to now is about the character of Christ being formed in us, the shaping process that comes and increases our abilities to contain the new wine of

His Spirit, without spilling it out on the ground. Impartation can be an event, but transformation is a process.

One of my favorite shows on television right now is *Gold Rush*, on the National Geographic Channel. I love that show! I particularly like the Hoffman crew. They are mining in the Klondike, having to break through frozen earth with a bulldozer and other heavy equipment. The processes that they have to go through to even have a chance to find gold are extraordinary. First they have to remove several feet of basically frozen mud—tons of it. Then, when they reach the material they call "pay dirt," they have to remove all of it, several feet down, to the bedrock. As they are removing the pay dirt, they feed that material through the wash plant, which, through vibration and a large flow of water, causes the heavier material—including the gold—to be separated and caught while the rest of the material washes out of the wash plant. Then they take the material that was caught and begin another process through another hopper that thoroughly separates the gold from the dirt that was trapped together in the wash plant. Usually, it's flakes of gold contained in tons of dirt. All the while they are doing this, equipment is breaking down, there's trouble back home, they are away from their families, and they are constantly reaching their breaking point.

My wife Christy laughs at me watching this show, and she said that it seems like so much work for what seems like a small amount of gold. But I realized while watching that show that it is such an illustration of the process of change in us. The treasure is in us—the earthen vessels. 2 Corinthians 4:7 says:

But we have this treasure in earthen vessels, so that the surpassing greatness of the power will be of God and not from ourselves...

When we are born again, the treasure of God is in us, but the mining out of that treasure requires the processes of life in the Spirit of God. He is building His character in us that will withstand the consuming fires and the test of time. Through the processes of God in our life experiences, He removes layers of useless weights and materials that the treasure is buried in, refining us in the process. Scripture uses examples of the threshing floor, where the wheat is separated from the chaff. That process happens individually and corporately among believers, and ultimately the nations of the earth. Thank God that He is the author and perfecter of our faith (Hebrews 12:2), and not us.

As believers, we are all learning to grow up in Christ, and I believe that the process is speeding up dramatically, because the revelation of Christ on the earth is exploding in people's hearts as never before. What took someone fifty years to mine out can be left to the next generation to enjoy the fruits of the previous generation's labors, with an elevated platform in the Spirit. The washing of the water of the Word strips away all the useless mud in our lives down to the pay dirt. "Pay dirt" is the material that gold miners love to get to, because that is where the gold is.

The useless mud in us is the bad thinking, lies, delusions, and strongholds of the enemy designed to choke out the living Word of God. As our minds are being renewed, God begins to reveal the unique treasure that He created us to be. His sifting process separates that which is precious from the useless. So now, it's no longer I that live, but Christ that lives in me (Galatians 2:20)!

CHAPTER 4

Come Just As You Are

When I was born again in 1982, I received Jesus on the basis that salvation was a free gift, that there was nothing I could do to earn it, and that I could come just like I was to receive it. If you've ever watched a Billy Graham crusade, at the end of the service, when the invitation is given, they sing the hymn, "Just As I Am." In some of our more contemporary evangelistic crusades, you may hear the song, "Come Just As You Are." Those songs reflect the truth that we can go to Jesus just like we are and receive His mercy and grace. The salvation we receive encompasses everything that pertains to life and Godliness. 2 Peter 1:2–4 (emphasis added) states:

Grace and peace be multiplied to you in the knowledge of God and of Jesus our Lord; seeing that His divine power has granted to us everything pertaining to life and godliness, through the true knowledge of Him who called us by His own glory and excellence. For by these He has granted to us His precious and magnificent promises, so that by them you may become partakers of **the** *divine nature, having escaped the corruption that is in the world by lust.*

This means redemption, righteousness, peace, joy, healing, blessings, and any other good thing from God was given to us through the undeserved favor by our faith in the knowledge of what Jesus accomplished on the cross. Wow, that's good news! As Larry the Cable Guy says, "That's good right there, I don't care who you are!" Ephesians 2:8–9 states:

For by grace you have been saved through faith; and that not of yourselves; it is the gift of God; not as a result of works, so that no one may boast.

So it's obvious according to Scripture that we cannot do anything to obtain righteousness through any works, from keeping the Ten Commandments to perfecting the law of sowing and reaping. Did you just gasp? Grace is defined as unmerited or undeserved favor. If we could obtain salvation by sowing for it, we would deserve it, according to what we have sown, and not our faith in the work of Jesus on the cross. I will speak more about this later in the book.

We must learn to live and move and have our being in Him, and we will, because He is the author and perfecter of our faith (Hebrews 12:2). When we live in Christ, we will sow good seed and bear good fruit. We can diligently seek Him, but we cannot sow our way into Him. His presence is His free gift to us, and we seek to live in His presence, which is free.

It is impossible to have an encounter with the true and living God without change occurring, either for the better or the worse. It's impossible to effectively live and move and have our being in Christ and not bear good fruit. If we are effectively living in Him, what we sow will be holy and acceptable to God, because it will be birthed from our communion with Him. It will not be because we are trying to work a religious system from our own reasoning that's hidden in the guise of some New Testament teaching. I am not saying the law of sowing and reaping doesn't exist and is not put into effect with everything we do. I'm saying my consciousness cannot be focused on my performance of any law; my focus has to be on where I'm living positionally. Am I living and moving and having my being in Him? Am I doing what I see Him do, and saying what I hear Him say? Is it no longer I that lives but Christ that lives in me? That's where my consciousness has to be. That's really where the good fight of faith is to be won or lost.

IN COMMUNION WITH GOD

When I use the term "effectively living in Him," I'm speaking of living in communion with God, by the free, undeserved gift we received from God. The accuser of the brethren, Satan and his entourage, comes to steal or choke out the word of God by making us conscious of where we are failing. He uses our imperfect performance to keep the law, or our low levels of obedience and discipline, to get us to believe that our performance is what prevents our salvation from fruition in our lives. Honestly, it's our lack of faith in the fact that Jesus's sacrifice on the cross was enough to make this positional place of rest and redemption possible.

When we add religious rules and formulas of men to what Jesus did, we are literally saying that what Jesus did on the cross was not enough. If we have fellowship with Jesus, it is sufficient. We will be, and demonstrate, His righteousness. When Jesus said, "It is finished," it truly was finished. The lie we swallow is now we are saved, so we need to start confessing Scripture, fasting, praying, tithing, offering, etc., to keep our salvation. So we put our focus on our works and off of our communion with God. In Matthew 6:33–34, Jesus states:

> *But seek first His kingdom and His righteousness, and all these things will be added to you. So do not worry about tomorrow; for tomorrow will care for itself. Each day has enough trouble of its own.*

> *Acts 17:28 (KJV) says, for in Him we live and move and have our being, as certain also of your own poets have said, For we are also His offspring.*

Communion with God begins when we receive Jesus as our Savior. When I think back to when I was born again, I just remember feeling so alive. I felt a divine sense of purpose with an unreasonable optimism. I could not get Jesus off my mind. Revelation seemed to be pouring in faster than I could retain it in the natural. I was in love and felt so free. Nothing seemed to matter—I had eternal life! My life began to change dramatically from the inside out. I still had issues some would call sin, others may call habits. Even though those things in my life made me uneasy at times, I was still consumed by the notion that Jesus had made me a new creation.

I was experiencing my first love. It was my initial encounter with Christ. Everything I thought or did was birthed from my love relationship with Christ. I soon received the Baptism of the Holy Spirit, and when that happened, things really took off. But as with most Christians over time, the feelings began to wane. As they did, I became more and more conscious of where I was not measuring up. What happened? I left my first love. In Galatians 3:1–3, Paul writes:

You foolish Galatians, who has bewitched you, before whose eyes Jesus Christ was clearly portrayed as crucified? This is the only thing I want to find out from you: did you receive the Spirit by the works of the Law, or by hearing with faith? Are you so foolish? Having begun by the Spirit, are you now being perfected by the flesh?

Ouch! *Selah.*

The more I tried to live what I was told was right, the more I seemed to fail. My consciousness was no longer on the "lover of my soul," but on myself and my perception of what was right and what was wrong. Self-consciousness can be interpreted as sin-consciousness when we begin to draw from the wrong well. We get the mindset that if we understand what sin is, then we can overcome it and change. But the truth is that understanding what sin is doesn't change us. (I will speak more on this subject later.)

AN ENCOUNTER WITH JESUS IS ALL THAT EVER WILL CHANGE ANYONE

I knew I was a sinner long before I knew who Jesus was. It is our encounter with Jesus that changes us. That's all that has ever changed anyone. That's all that ever *will* change anyone. That's why He says that there is no other way to the Father except through Him. We can read Scripture for hours every day and still not be in communion with Him.

We can pray for hours and hours and not be in communion with Christ. The purpose for doing these things was never meant to take the place of a living relationship with Christ (John 5:39–40).

Doing all the things that seem right to man doesn't make me a good guy or right with God. Scripture says there is a way that seems right to a man that in the end leads to death (Proverbs 14:12). So, I can't bear the fruits of the Spirit just because I'm a good guy, go to church, and believe in Jesus. I can only bear good fruit after conceiving life by the Spirit of God through Christ Jesus. For example, if a man gets married and comes together with his wife in the natural, then the two become one. Because they come together, the potential is there for conception, whether the wife is virtuous or not. If there are no health problems or abnormalities, then she will conceive and ultimately give birth to the life produced, as the result of their communion. When a woman is giving birth, we call it labor, so her good works are the birthing of the life produced through her communion with her husband. You see, I can *believe* I have a wife but unless I *commune* with her through becoming one flesh, she will not *conceive* a child.

In the same way, when we commune with God, we conceive life. Our labor or works are to bear the fruit of the life that we conceived through our communion. Every significant thing we do, pertaining to our life in Christ, should be birthed from our communion with Him. That's why Jesus said, "I only do what I see my Father do, and I only say what I hear my Father say" (John 5:19; John 12:49). He only spoke the words conceived through His communion with the Father. Wow! *Selah.*

Writing this book is the labor process for giving birth to what I've been carrying for the appointed time. I hope what is birthed from my communion with God will be able to stand the test of fire, and not all will be destroyed. As a songwriter, when I'm worshipping God, an idea for a song may pop into my mind. Now I must labor to give birth to the inspired idea, by letting the idea develop, and then by putting the words to music. Those are our works. James 2:17–18 states:

> *Even so faith, if it has no works, is dead, being by itself. But someone may well say, "You have faith and I have works; show me your faith without the works, and I will show you my faith by my works."*

Some people may believe that their works speak for themselves, but I believe our works will speak for who Jesus truly is, or they will speak for whatever our agenda is. In other words, we may be using our works to exalt ourselves, or even a distorted perception of Christianity. We are supposed to humble ourselves. The most important exaltation we need to desire is what comes from God alone. From the overflowing cup of our communion with God, we encourage people, help people, teach, clothe, visit, bless, heal, write, sing, turn over money changers' tables, smile, laugh, weep, love, forgive—those works show our faith in what Jesus accomplished through His death, burial, and resurrection. They will know we're His disciples because we love one another (John 13:35). In John 15:1–5, Jesus states:

> *"I am the true vine, and My Father is the vinedresser. Every branch in Me that does not bear fruit, He takes away; and every branch that bears fruit, He prunes it so that it may bear more fruit. You are already clean because of the word which I have spoken to you. Abide in Me, and I in you. As the branch cannot bear fruit of itself unless it abides in the vine, so neither can you unless you abide in Me. I am the vine, you are the branches; he who*

abides in Me and I in him, he bears much fruit, for apart from Me you can do nothing."

This Scripture about abiding in the vine is absolutely an illustration of communion and the process of birthing or bearing the works of our faith or the fruits of the Spirit.

The greatest treasure that we can possess, as Christians on this earth, is our holy communion with God: the Father, the Son, and the Holy Ghost. He is the prize. To Him, we owe our lives. By Him, we were purchased with the blood of His only Son. He alone knows our beginning and our end on this earth, and He alone is the author and perfecter of our faith. He alone is good. He is holy, and my soul longs for Him. Nothing is more wonderful than to experience His presence and to hear His voice. Nothing begins to compare with His incredible love and grace.

We will marvel at the mystery of His love and grace for all eternity and never reach the ends of it. He is the great Redeemer. At His slightest move, waves of light and life flow over us. He is our lover, and we are His. His grace to us will not be overcome. Nothing will separate us from His love! He is love! Satan has been defeated, and his lies are being brought to nothing. Our love for God is torture to the eyes of the prideful. God himself resists the proud and gives grace to the humble (1 Peter 5:5). Therefore, let us humble ourselves in the sight of our Lord and He will lift us up (James 4:10)! Let His rod and staff comfort us (Psalm 23:4). Glory to God and Him alone. Indeed, let God be true and every man be a liar (Romans 3:4).

Communion with God has many levels and diversities. It can be in the form of His manifest presence (John 14:21), His still small voice (1 Kings 19:12), through worship, friends, preaching, teaching, prophetic utterance, prayer—a host of ways not exclusive to or limited to these examples. Jesus said, *"My sheep know My voice"* (John 10:27, paraphrased). Even when we feel miles away, He is there, and when we are weak, He is strong. Our job is to keep our hearts turned to Him in all that life brings. That is when we grow deep roots in Him.

I do not want to sound as if I have arrived, because I have failed in these areas over and over, just like everyone else. If I thought I had arrived, then I would no longer be in need of His grace. Our salvation is because of grace. What Jesus did on the cross through His death, burial, and resurrection is the only leg I have to stand on. What He did on the cross, and my faith in that work, is the only thing that will ever justify me. In John 6:54–58, Jesus states:

> *"He who eats My flesh and drinks My blood has eternal life, and I will raise him up on the last day. For My flesh is true food, and My blood is true drink. He who eats My flesh and drinks My blood abides in Me, and I in him. As the living Father sent Me, and I live because of the Father, so he who eats Me, he also will live because of Me. This is the bread which came down out of heaven; not as the fathers ate and died; he who eats this bread will live forever."*

There is a communion that happens corporately, within the church. We commune with God when a person ministers under the anointing, through worship, and through our fellowship with each other. When Jesus said we must eat His body and drink His blood, I believe we must look also at who He says is His body. Those who have called on the name of the Lord and have been saved are the body of Christ on this earth. In 1 Corinthians 12:27, Paul is speaking to the church at Corinth, and he says, *Now you are Christ's body, and individually members of it.*

WE MUST PREFER ONE ANOTHER MORE THAN OURSELVES

We not only eat the word of God Himself through our individual communion with Him but we also must be able to receive from each other without rivalries, jealousies, envious hearts, and the like. We must prefer one another more than ourselves. When we get mad with a brother, we no longer partake of that part of the body of Christ. We love to go to the throne of grace for ourselves, but we sometimes resist being a place of grace for others. The world, as well as the doctrines and traditions of men, works hard to expose people, but love covers a multitude of sin (1 Peter 4:8).

In Genesis 9:18–28, there is the story of Noah getting drunk and lying naked in his tent. His youngest son Ham saw his father's condition and went out and told his two brothers about it. But when Shem and Japheth heard this, they got a blanket, put it over their shoulders and backed up to Noah so they wouldn't look upon his nakedness. When Noah awakened, he knew what Ham had done, and he made Ham's son Canaan the servant of Shem and Japheth and blessed them for covering his nakedness.

Love covers our nakedness. We must learn to love each other at this level to achieve the communion God designed for us. Our communion with each other will be a great feast to us if we will love one another and bear one another's faults through being graceful, remembering where we came from, or perhaps where we presently are.

When we partake in a communion service, we use small pieces of bread that represent His body broken for us and juice or wine that represents His blood shed for us. Jesus instructed His disciples to "do this in remembrance of Me." He says His blood represents the new covenant, and He describes his body as being given for us (Luke 22:19–20). Obviously, the bread and juice imply more than a snack! In Matthew 4:4, Jesus is speaking to his disciples and states:

> *But He answered and said, "It is written, 'Man shall not live on bread alone, but on every word that proceeds out of the mouth of God.'"*

Notice the word "proceeds"; that is present tense. We don't live on what God said, but what God is saying to us now! When you read what Jesus said two thousand years ago, you may hear Him speaking a *now* word that edifies or strengthens you in your circumstances. You may hear Him speak a word of wisdom or knowledge for someone else, or He may impart instructions to you that we are to be obedient to. We need to presently hear His voice.

CHAPTER 5

The Sheep and the Goats

So, who were the sheep and the goats? In my younger years, I always thought that the sheep were those who were for and professed Christ, and the goats were those who were against Him. However, as I grew in the Lord and began to study these passages, many unexpected things jumped at me. I want to start this chapter with the story of the sheep and the goats as depicted in Scripture, and you may be amazed at what is discovered. In Matthew 25:31–46, Jesus says:

> *"But when the Son of Man comes in His glory, and all the angels with Him, then He will sit on His glorious throne. All the nations will be gathered before Him; and He will separate them one from another, as a shepherd separates the sheep from the goats; and He will put the sheep on His right, and the goats on the left.*
>
> *"Then the King will say to those on His right, 'Come, you who are blessed of My Father, inherit the kingdom prepared for you from the*

foundation of the world. For I was hungry, and you gave Me something to eat; I was thirsty, and you gave Me something to drink; I was a stranger, and you invited Me in; naked and you clothed Me; I was sick, and you visited Me; I was in prison, and you came to Me.' Then the righteous will answer Him, 'Lord, when did we see You hungry, and feed You, or thirsty, and give You something to drink? And when did we see You a stranger, and invite You in, or naked, and clothe You? When did we see You sick, or in prison, and come to You?' The King will answer and say to them, 'Truly I say to you, to the extent that you did it to one of these brothers of mine, even the least of them, you did it to Me.'

"Then He will also say to those on His left, 'Depart from Me, accursed ones, into the eternal fire which has been prepared for the devil and his angels; for I was hungry, and you gave Me nothing to eat; I was thirsty, and you gave Me nothing to drink; I was a stranger, and you did not invite Me in; naked, and you did not clothe Me; sick, and in prison, and you did not visit Me.' Then they themselves also will answer, 'Lord, when did we see You hungry, or thirsty, or a stranger, or naked, or sick, or in prison, and did not take care of You?' Then He will answer them, 'Truly, I say to you, to the extent that you did not do it to one of the least of these, you did not do it to Me.' These will go away into eternal punishment, but the righteous into eternal life."

Those are very heavy and sobering words, and even as I was writing those references, I could sense the deep sadness of the Lord. He was not proudly saying, "I'll show you." He's just describing what will happen to men who reject Him. It is a tragedy for any man to miss what God has done for him. Yet sadly, if men continue to reject Him, these things will happen just as He spoke that they would.

When a man is condemned to death in our court system, on the day of the execution, everyone who participates in the process of his execution feels the extraordinary weight of it. No one is laughing. There is a fear and trembling for all involved at the moment of execution, in many cases even for the families of the condemned man's victims.

Now, these Scriptures indicate that, when Jesus returns in His glory, there will be a judgment of the nations and that He will separate the sheep from the goats. Most anyone who would read that would think He is referring to the separation of believers from nonbelievers. In a sense, that is true. But read Jesus's words in Matthew 7:21–23:

> *"Not everyone who says to Me, 'Lord, Lord,' will enter the kingdom of heaven, but he who does the will of My Father who is in heaven will enter. Many will say to Me on that day, 'Lord, Lord, did we not prophesy in Your name, and in Your name cast out demons, and in Your name perform many miracles? And then I will declare to them, 'I never knew you; depart from Me, you who practice lawlessness!'"*

KNOW HIM PERSONALLY

Obviously, not everyone who says they are His knows Jesus. That is why it is crucial that we know Him personally. It's not what you know; it's who you know. So, based on the whole counsel of all we have just read, the sheep are those believers who know Jesus personally. The goats are those who are either unbelievers or those who *say* they know Him, when in fact they do not. Remember the Proverb, *There is a way which seems right to a man, but its end is the way of death* (Proverbs 14:12). It is not enough to believe in Jesus; Satan believes in Jesus, yet has nothing in common with Him. Read what Jesus told the Pharisees in John 9:38–41:

> *And he said, "Lord, I believe!" And he worshiped Him. And Jesus said, "For judgment I came into this world, so that those who do not see may see, and that those who see may become blind." Those of the Pharisees who*

were with Him heard these things, and said to Him, "We are not blind too, are we?" Jesus said to them, "If you were blind, you would have no sin; but since you say, 'We see,' your sin remains."

These particular goats are those who say they see, yet do not see; who claim their vision is clear, yet they judge and reject those who appear to be poor, miserable, blind, and naked. When Pharisees and religious-spirited people see the poor, miserable, blind, and naked, Jesus sees "the least of these." When Jesus sees the poor, miserable, blind, and naked, often times, if not most, He is looking at religious-spirited people with hearts full of pride.

I found it so profound that Jesus was exalting the works of the sheep, and their attitude is, "Lord, when did we do these things?" But it was their attitude in this portion of Scripture that really illuminates a lot of the revelation that has been threaded throughout this book. They were unconscious of their good works because they weren't trying to accomplish their righteousness through their works. They were just being themselves, enjoying life, living and moving and having their being in Him. They knew they had no works to justify themselves; they only had the grace extended to them by Jesus through the finished work on the cross. Their focus wasn't on having good works; it's just who they were. The result was that the love in their hearts enabled them to express good works!

The contrast for the sheep's reaction is the goats'. Again, by the whole counsel of what we have read, the goats are the ones who didn't make it. They were referred to as "cursed" and those "He never knew, who practice lawlessness." I find it profound how they responded to Jesus when He was rebuking them by saying, "Lord, we prophesied in

Your name, we cast out devils in Your name, and did many signs and wonders in Your name" (paraphrased). Now, does that sound like justification to you? They were, in essence, saying, "We have a right to be here!"

Now, think about it. You have just been rebuked by the Creator of the universe. All of His holy angels are staring at you, and even then you would try to justify your place in the Kingdom. That is pride, and that is why Lucifer was kicked out of heaven. Our sin has been dealt with on the cross, but we have to deal with our pride.

HIS SHEEP KNOW HIS VOICE

I also noticed that the sheep's focus was helping those in dire need, and the goats who said they were believers found justification in their spiritual gifting with the signs and wonders they performed. Is this scary to you? Do not be afraid; if you are determined in your heart to know Him, then He will make himself known to you. If you are hearing His voice in what I am writing, relax. You already know Him, because He said His sheep know His voice, even if you are identifying more with the goats than you are with the sheep. We are in the days of grace, and with one tweak of your heart, you can know Him personally. Just humble yourself before the Lord and ask. He loves you.

> *"I know your deeds, that you are neither cold nor hot; I wish you were cold or hot. So because you are lukewarm, and neither hot nor cold, I will spit you out of My mouth. Because you say, "I am rich, and have become wealthy, and have need of nothing," and you do not know that you are wretched and miserable and poor and blind and naked, I advise you to buy from Me gold refined by fire so that you may become rich; and white*

garments so that you may clothe yourself, and that the shame of your nakedness may not be revealed; and eye salve to anoint your eyes so that you may see."'

~ Revelation 3:15–18

CHAPTER 6

Love

All things are lawful for me, but not all things are not profitable. All things are lawful for me, but I will not be mastered by any.

~ 1 Corinthians 6:12

You may be asking, "What does this Scripture have to do with love?" I believe that, the more we discover God's intent for us, the deeper understanding we have of His nature. This Scripture reflects that we have been set free from the law. In other words, we can do anything we want. It doesn't qualify all things in any way. It could seem as if God is saying, "There you go, boys and girls, you are free! Now you can choose to do anything you want, whether I like it or not." But is that really the heart of God, or actually a platform created for us to choose from?

When Adam was created, he was free to do anything. He could literally do anything he wanted. Nothing was off the table; there were no holds barred, because nothing he could do would give him a sin consciousness. He did whatever he chose. But God wanted to establish something in him—something even more precious than all he was given. Adam had dominion over everything, every bird in the sky, creeping crawling things, the earth itself was his to rule. But there was one thing the Lord wanted to increase in Adam that could only be accomplished in one way. So the Lord put before him a test. You could call it a test, **or an opportunity**. It was a choice—a choice he didn't have to make before this moment. God brought him into the Garden of Eden, and showed Adam all that He had provided for him and said Adam could eat from any of the trees except this one tree—the Tree of the Knowledge of Good and Evil.

After He showed Adam the garden, God saw that it was not good for Adam to be alone, so He created Eve. Adam and Eve lived in the garden as God instructed, yet the test to accomplish something greater still remained. It was this one thing God told them not to do, always there in front of them. I'm sure they stared at it and scratched their heads, thinking, why would God allow this tree, that will kill us if we eat from it, to live in this garden?

Then Eve is confronted by a serpent. The serpent tempted her to eat from the forbidden tree. Genesis 3:1 speaks about this serpent, and that it was more cunning than any beast of the field. The serpent basically told her, "The reason God does not want you to eat from this tree, is because He knows If you eat from this tree, you'll be like Him; knowing what is good and evil" (paraphrased). So this creates another question. If God created everything and saw that it was good, why was the serpent tempting Eve? Here are two clues.

And He said to them, "I was watching Satan fall from heaven like lightning."

~ Luke 10:18

"How you have fallen from heaven,
O star of the morning, son of the dawn!
You have been cut down to the earth,
You who weakened the nations!
"But you said in your heart,
'I will ascend to heaven;
I will raise my throne above the stars of God,
And I will sit on the mount of assembly
In the recesses of the north.
'I will ascend above the heights of the clouds;
I will make myself like the Most High.'"

~ Isaiah 14:12–14

The Scriptures say the serpent was the most cunning of all the beasts of the field. Satan knew that, and had obviously already corrupted him. So, it is clear to me that Satan was on the earth when God created everything and saw that the earth was good. Why would God do that with Satan still on the earth? It's the same as putting a forbidden tree in the middle of the Garden of Eden. There is a lot of mystery in this story, but I want to focus on something that seems to be jumping out at me. Adam was described as a living soul, alive by the breath of God. Scripture says God is love, and God gave of Himself to create Adam. Every day, Adam would see the forbidden tree, and remember what God had said, and obey. When he did this, he would become stronger in spirit, increased with wisdom, and grace would be upon him. You might say he didn't need grace, because grace is for imperfect people. However, Jesus was perfect in all of His ways.

> *The Child continued to grow and become strong, increasing in wisdom;* **and the grace of God was upon Him.**

~ Luke 2:40 (emphasis added)

Jesus was called the second Adam in Scripture. So, grace is far more than unmerited favor. Adam was created by God, and he was of God— perfect in all of his ways. However, without the opportunity for Adam to choose between disobedience and obedience, there was no way for him to establish and prove his love for the Father. Lucifer was created by God, and he was created perfect, but he didn't choose to remain perfect. Since God looked at His creation, and saw that it was good, then the serpent wasn't evil to begin with. When the serpent ate the bait of Satan, he became the slave to that which he obeyed. He was taken captive by the enemy to do his will. 2 Timothy 2:26 speaks of men who have been taken captive by the enemy to do his will.

PARTAKERS OF HIS DIVINE NATURE

God is perfect and has all power in heaven and earth. He has always been perfect. He's not perfect just because He has always been perfect—He's perfect because He chooses to be perfect. The difference is God, who is perfect to love, *chose* love. God was obedient to His own identity. When most of us think of obedience, we think only in the terms of obeying the authority over us. But what if obedience is actually a lot more than that? 2 Peter 1:4 says, *we are partakers of His divine nature* (paraphrased).

Now we hear His voice and we do what He says, but we are not only being obedient to Him, we are being obedient to someone else—our own divine nature. We are choosing to be who He says we are. That's why our identity of who we are in Him is so important. When we are being obedient to who we are, we are taking ownership of our identity. Jesus took ownership of His identity. That's why, when those who came to arrest Him asked if He was Jesus, they fell backwards when He said, "I AM." Taking ownership releases the power of God in us and reflects the divine nature that we are partakers of. When we are obedient to Christ, our own identity increases. That truly is being true to ourselves.

Now I want to talk about the real threat to our identity. It's elusive in nature and seeks to blindside us. It sneaks up on us, it's crafty in all its ways, and it's deceptive in nature. It bears the fruit of disobedience in every form. Preachers can have it, bank robbers, murderers, adulterers, musicians, doctors, lawyers, thieves, apostles, prophets, evangelists, pastors, teachers, Republicans, Democrats,—everyone is the target of this culprit. What is the evil thing? What could do all this? It is that thing that got Lucifer kicked out of Heaven. It is *pride*.

PRIDE SEEKS ITS OWN

It is pride that causes men to fall. Pride comes before a fall. Pride chooses its own desires over the ways of love. Pride seeks its own. Love does not seek its own. Love humbles itself under the mighty hand of God. To choose God, we must humble ourselves. Pride inflates itself. When we operate in pride, we inflate ourselves. To be proud is to be poor, miserable, blind, and naked. It is pride that distorts knowledge.

When Adam realized he was naked, it is because he now saw things through the distortion of his own pride—he now had knowledge. Not *revelation* knowledge, but the knowledge of his own reasoning.

When Eve was tempted, she was tempted to have the ability to be like God. She was tempted to have what she was already designed to be. But she didn't trust that God wanted those things for her, so she ate the fruit of disobedience, because pride seeks its own desires. Adam was responsible for all that happened because he had authority to put a stop to it. But he didn't, because his own desire to be like God was enticed by his pride; therefore, he disobeyed. He was already designed to be like God, but to truly be like God, he had to choose not to seek his own will. Jesus, the second Adam, in the Garden of Gethsemane, said, *"Father not my will, but Your will be done"* (Luke 22:42, paraphrased). That is humility, the antithesis of pride. God dealt with sin and death, but He tells us to humble ourselves.

> *Humble yourselves in the presence of the Lord, and He will exalt you.*
>
> ~ James 4:10

> *But He gives a greater grace. Therefore it says, "God is opposed to the proud, but gives grace to the humble."*
>
> ~ James 4:6

So, God doesn't want to take away a person's right to *choose*, because that is His gift to them. He said, *"If you eat from this tree, you will surely die"* (Genesis 2:17b, paraphrased). In other words, God was acknowledging that, they could make the choice to eat from that tree, when He said the word, "If." He's basically saying, "I'm just telling you if you eat from it, you will die." God wanted them to follow the way of love—to choose love.

"If you love Me, you will keep My commandments."

~ John 14:15

The test was their opportunity to humble themselves and *choose* love. God Himself is love, and He wanted them to follow the way of love. The way of love is humility. When you choose to follow God, you follow love and you walk in humility. If you are walking in pride, you're not walking in love. If there is no opportunity to choose anything else other than love, then making the choice to follow God wouldn't be love. When you choose not to choose disobedience, you have chosen love. Love chooses to obey, and not serve anything else but God. To choose anything else would not be love. Love is God's heart. He loved the world so much that He chose to give His only begotten Son. He gave because He loved.

CHOOSE LOVE AND WALK IN LOVE

God's intent, when He created Adam and Eve, was that they would *choose* love and walk in love. God wanted Adam to be true to, and be established in, his own identity—who he was created to be. God first chose us to follow Him. When Jesus died on the cross and was resurrected, God's intent for us was to be those who would choose Jesus, and live in Him. The facts are that Jesus destroyed the law of sin and death; all things are now lawful. Now all men can choose to love. No matter what condition they are in, or what they have done, they can now choose Jesus. When you choose Jesus, you choose love. Obviously, things look a lot different to us in the natural realm than it did for Adam and Eve. When we are born again, in spite of the obvious contradictions, in many ways we are as Adam and Eve were before the fall, if you have eyes to see. Before Jesus, we were all doomed for hell; there was no other choice to be made. Now we have a choice. Adam and Eve lived where they had a choice; we now live where we have a choice. Sin and death are destroyed, but here is the paradox that does make our situation different than Adam and Eve's. There was no law of sin and death, unless they disobeyed, and they were not in a fallen condition before they were disobedient. With us, we were already in a fallen condition, but there is no life unless we receive Christ.

Now, even though sin and death were destroyed on the cross, until you become born again, you are still under the fallen perception of the Tree of the Knowledge of Good and Evil. You must be born again to receive the perception that comes from the Tree of Life. So, God is saying, you are free to do what you want; I no longer hold that against you. However, Jesus said that, if you want eternal life with Me, you must eat My flesh and drink My blood. In other words, you must eat from this one tree, the Tree of Life! So now, if we go to hell, it will not be because of sin; it will be because we reject Christ. Men do not go to hell because they sin. All of God's anger and wrath towards sin and death were put upon Jesus, for all mankind, and our sin was nailed to the cross. Men go to hell because they reject the One who came to set them free from their fallen perception and the bondage that enslaves them. If we desire to be enslaved by anything other than our Father's love, we will literally be choosing hell for ourselves. Before Christ, we had no hope for eternal life, we were doomed to our fallen nature and the law against it, because the law of sin and death reigned over us. However, when we are introduced to the Gospel of Christ, it is the same as when God introduced Adam and Eve to the garden. God told them to not eat from this one forbidden tree. Now He is telling us to eat the bread of life and drink the living waters of this One man—Jesus! Now, in order to be pleasing to God, and true to ourselves, we must choose love Himself. To love is Christ.

Now I want to show you the polar opposite of the story in the garden. It's the story of Jesus's temptation:

Then Jesus was led up by the Spirit into the wilderness to be tempted by the devil. And after He had fasted forty days and forty nights, He then became hungry. And the tempter came and said to Him, "If You are the Son of God, command that these stones become bread." But He answered and said, "It is written, 'Man shall not live on bread alone, but by every word that proceeds out of the mouth of God.'"

Then the devil took Him into the holy city and had Him stand on the pinnacle of the temple, and said to Him, "If You are the Son of God, throw Yourself down; for it is written: 'He will command His angels concerning You,' and, 'On their hands they will bear You up, So that You will not strike Your foot against a stone.'"

Jesus said to him, "On the other hand, it is written, 'You shall not put the Lord your God to the test.'"

Again, the devil took Him up to a very high mountain and showed Him all the kingdoms of the world and their glory; and he said to Him, "All these things I will give You, if You fall down and worship me." Then Jesus said to him, "Go, Satan! For it is written, 'You shall worship the Lord your God, and serve Him only.'" Then the devil left Him; and behold, angels came and began to minister to Him."

~ Matthew 4:1–10

Adam was told by God all this was his, everything he saw. *Just don't do this one thing*—do not eat from the forbidden tree. When Jesus was tempted, Satan was the ruler of the earth, and he told Jesus, "I'll give you all this, everything You see if You will do this one thing—fall down and worship me" (paraphrased). And though Jesus was perfect in all His ways, in that moment, He still had to choose the way of love! How do I know this? Because the Scripture, says He was tempted. To be tempted is to have a desire to have something. It was a natural desire for Jesus to have everything He was shown, because He was created to have it. James 1:14 says, *But each one is tempted when he is carried away and enticed by his own lust* (emphasis added). So for Jesus to have it by rite of passage, or legally, He had to choose love. It was His love for His Father, and His love for us, that enabled Him to be obedient, even unto death. Wow! Now all those kingdoms and nations Satan showed Him are His, by right. What an incredible love.

LOVE GIVES BIRTH TO ETERNAL LIFE

One of the greatest revelations a person can have is that God loves us just like we are. But I believe it is God's desire for us to love Him just like He is. Even God wants to be loved for who He is. When, in the midst of all the chaos and confusion there is in this world, we choose God, and His ways of love, we bless His heart. Now we are free, and He doesn't see our sin, He sees our *choice*. When we choose to believe in the finished work of the cross for our salvation, our faith is accounted to us as righteousness.

Had Adam and Eve made the choice to choose God, who is Love Himself, and had chosen not to disobey, they would have chosen to make Love Himself their Lord, by their own choosing. They would have been true to who they were created to be. They would have humbled themselves and increased in wisdom and stature. More grace would have been upon them. The love of God would have governed everything they did. He was already Lord, but they couldn't make Him *their* Lord unless they made the choice to love. They would have chosen to become one with the Father, just as Jesus and the Father are one. His love would have been the motivating factor behind everything they did. The love of God would have fulfilled their purpose in life. They would have eaten the fruit of obedience, rather than the fruit of their disobedience. Love gives birth to eternal life. Sin gives birth to death.

LOVE

Since the Father and the Son are One, and both are God, and God is Love, then Love was made flesh, and He dwelt awhile among us. And while Love was on the earth, He was about His Father's business. Love turned water into wine at a wedding. One day, Love Himself was led into the wilderness by the Spirit of Love to be tempted by the evil one. The evil one showed Love all Love could have if He would bow His knee to him. But Love chose Love and when Love returned, Love returned in power. Love raised Lazarus from the dead. Love healed the sick and cast devils out of people. Love made a whip and turned over the moneychanger's tables. Love told the Pharisees they couldn't understand Love Himself because they were of their father, the Devil. Love hated sin, but He loved sinners.

There are no laws against Love either, so He walked on water, defying the law of gravity. Because there are no laws against Love, the disciples of Love gathered wheat on the Sabbath, defying what was lawful according to man on the Sabbath. Love fed five thousand men with five loaves and two fishes. The Pharisees and Sadducees were suspicious of Love. They wanted to know who gave Love His authority, but Love wouldn't tell them, because Love doesn't answer to men. The Pharisees and Sadducees could not recognize Love. But the tax collectors, the prostitutes, the demon possessed, the sick, the poor, the blind, and even a dead man named Lazarus could see Love, and recognized Love's voice was from above. They loved Love and would do anything Love asked of them.

But ultimately, we took Love and we made a mockery out of Love, but that was only to ourselves, because Love will not be mocked. We beat Love until He was unrecognizable and put a crown of thorns on the head of Love. Then we nailed Love to the cross, and we laughed at Love scornfully and said, "This is what we think about Your Love." Love said, "Forgive them, Father, for they know not what they do." Then Love said, "It is finished." Now Love was dead; so they took Love's body and put it into a tomb.

The Pharisees had heard Love say that He would rise again in three days. So they sent their soldiers to seal up the tomb and to guard it. I guess they didn't want Love to break out. But Love did break out! On the third day, there was a great earthquake and an angel of Love descended, rolled away the stone, and Love was alive. Love had conquered the law of sin and death, because there are no laws against Love. Now any man who calls on the name of Love will be born of Love. They will be a new creature in Love. It is so good to be in Love! Love said we will do greater things than He did.

Before Love ascended, Love told them to wait in Jerusalem and not do anything else until they got the promise of Love. After saying these things, Love ascended to His Father and sat down at His right hand. Now Love is ever interceding for us. Love is our advocate with the Father, who is Love.

While the men of Love were waiting for the promise, as Love asked them to, they were all praying to Love in one accord. Then the Spirit of Love descended upon them all! One of the men of Love stood up preaching, and three thousand people chose Love. Now Love was everywhere, and daily more people chose Love. Love was pleased each time this happened. Love gave gifts to these men of Love, to help establish the government of Love in the men of Love. Love governs His government, because Love Himself is the chief cornerstone. Love warned His government to be careful how they built upon the foundation of Love, because He is Love, and whatever is built upon Love must be in Love.

Now these men of Love choose to Love daily. Some of these men of Love died for choosing Love, but their reward was great, and they did it for the joy of Love on the other side. Men of Love face many challenges in life, but when they choose Love, they take a higher place of dominion. Sometimes the men of Love feel that they don't measure up to Love, but Love tells them the grace of Love makes up the difference, and Love covers their multitude of sin. Love says to rest in His Love. The men of Love are questioned often about who gives them their authority to Love, but Love doesn't have to answer to men. Men, however, will one day answer to Love, and some of those will say they chose Love, but Love will say, I never knew you. Now that all these things have happened, Love cannot be stopped! This earth seems lost, but Love never fails, and ultimately Love wins! So choose Love and spread the love of Love.

Wow, what you just read just happened spontaneously. I did not plan it. I immediately backed it up on my flash drive, because I didn't want to take the chance of losing it! I believe the Lord wanted to use this allegory of using the word love in the place of Jesus or God for two reasons. The first reason is foundational, because everything we do now should be motivated by love. To put it another way, when we live in Christ and hear His voice, we hear the voice of love—and that we obey, by choice. The second reason is to challenge our perception of *what* and *who* love really is. If using the word love seems to cheapen who God is, it's because our perception of love has been tainted by the influence of the forbidden tree. For instance, sometimes we think that we should never do anything that would offend anyone, and that would be true, if there is no purpose for it. But if you walked in that perception of love alone, you would diminish Love's capacity to confront injustice. The truth is, love offends some people.

LIFE IN CHRIST IS NOW

Take, for instance, the popular "What Would Jesus Do" bracelet. The things Jesus did were profound and confounded the wise. So, if we live by our own perceptions of what's good and evil, then we will misrepresent Jesus. The fact is we will be doing what *we* think He would do, and not what *He* is saying to do. Life in Christ is a *now event*, taking place *presently* and drawing us into our future constantly. That is what eternal life does. We are learning to grow up into this new creation we were created to be. We must learn to live by the word that proceeds out of His mouth presently.

> *"I can do nothing on My own initiative. As I hear, I judge; and My judgment is just, because I do not seek My own will, but the will of Him who sent Me."*

> ~ John 5:30

So, what would Jesus do? He would judge as He hears. As He hears what? The voice of Him who sent Him. Why? Because He does not seek His own, but the will of His Father who sent Him. Love never seeks its own. So it is not enough to function out of our conclusions of Him. When we conclude, we begin to assume and call it discernment, when in fact it is our own reasoning. It is this kind of way that seems right to a man that in the end brings death. Scripture says trust in God with all your

78

heart and lean not on your on understanding (Proverbs 3:5). So, what tree is your perception grafted into?

We do not speak from what we think; we speak from what we know. You could say we speak from *Whom* we know, because we do not seek our own will but the will of Him who sends us. We choose love. When we *know* we are not our own, we have the full authority to *own* what we know. To *know* is to *own*. You cannot fully walk in what you *think* you know, because you do not *know* what you are thinking. Until you *know* what you are thinking, you do not own it. You can only give what you have, not what you *think* you have. By faith you have it, but faith must pass into revelation knowledge before you possess what you believe for. You must know it is yours presently. How do you know when you own it? Because you choose love, and you bear the fruit of Him who chose you. You rest in the fact that what you believe for is yours. You bear the fruits of the Spirit.

Jesus said, "They will know you're my disciples because you love one another" (John 13:35, paraphrased). Now, when you walk in the knowing, it's not like the Pharisees who say they see. Jesus told them that, because they say they see, their sin remains. If you walk in the *knowing* of Him, you should *know* to remain a novice at heart. You should *know* that you do not know it all. It pleases God for others to be able to tell us something that we do not know about Him. There is nothing worse than trying to teach a room full of *know-it-alls*. *Know-it-alls* are not walking in the heart of the One who knows all things.

There is no greater love than to lay down your life for your friends. Jesus did that for us because He *knew* who He was. Jesus manifests Himself to those who abide in Him. Our revelation and dispensation of

Love Himself will build the church: not by the hands of men, but by the Spirit of God; not by the sweat of men's brow, which was of the curse, but by the Spirit of Truth; not the truth perceived by men, but the imparted truth by God. It is the Kingdom of God that will flourish and replenish the earth, not the networks of men. The Kingdom of Heaven is not divided. It is people who are divided.

THE LEAVEN OF THE PHARISEES AND HEROD

The suspicions of men divide men, and they exclude everyone they are suspicious of. That is the leaven of the Pharisees and Herod, who are a law unto their own suspicious selves. They were not mindful of the things of God then, and they are not mindful of the things of God now. They are mindful of the things of men. They choose the elite when God chooses the afflicted. They choose the rich when God chooses the poor. They say they see, yet they are blind; we know we are blind, yet we see. In John 9:41 (NIV), Jesus says, *"If you were blind, you would not be guilty of sin; but now that you claim you can see, your guilt remains."* They say they are reigning as kings; we say as Paul in 1 Corinthians 4:8, when he was chiding those who had twisted the gospel, "We wish you really were reigning as kings; then we would be reigning with you" (paraphrased). The Kingdom is not divided, but men are divided. The things of men are carnal; the things of God are Spirit and life to those who find them. Let those who hear, hear what the Spirit is saying. Let those who are ignorant remain ignorant. What I'm speaking into is this: all who are in Christ should be of one mind and one spirit. That is what this is referring to. If one reigns, all reign. When one suffers, all suffer. The leaven of the Pharisees and Herod blinds and divides.

"Now the whirlwind is in the thorn tree." That's a line from a Johnny Cash song that has been speaking to me. Sometimes we feel like we are living in a thorn tree, and the sufferings can be devastating. However, Scripture says that Jesus learned obedience through His sufferings. Sometimes we hear the whirlwind speak the clearest in the thorn tree. The Lord spoke to Job from a whirlwind. Job was definitely living in a thorn tree, metaphorically speaking. God wants us to be blessed. I'm sure of that, but our definitions of blessing and success are not the same as God's.

For example, I would have never chosen to go through what I have been through. I fought it tooth and nail, to no avail. I thought I was destroyed. But it's very important to know who God is, even in those situations. Your circumstances may not define who God is, but God will always define Himself in your circumstances if you look for Him. It is important to know God in diverse situations. I would not trade anything for what I have been able to learn about God through the situations my family and I have endured. Yes, the same situations where I wanted to die. Because of them, I now have a greater level of mercy and grace toward others and myself that I didn't possess before. I've learned obedience through my sufferings.

It amazes me that Paul wrote much of his teaching while he was imprisoned. He was boasting in the Lord and boasting of his freedom while chained to a Roman soldier! That makes what he wrote all the more profound. I'm so glad God put it in my heart to write this book now. In the natural, there are a lot of things that remain the same. I am still in a limited financial prison myself, yet I feel like I possess all things. This is the supernatural power of God at work in me, and I feel so privileged to get to do this. I'm so thankful to God for the treasure I found in this place, that He has allowed me to glean all I can from this experience.

I sense that things will soon change in our lives for the better, circumstantially, perhaps from writing this book. I don't know. But I'm glad for me and for you that I am a living testimony that you can have peace in the storm. As for me, "storm" is a much too nice a word for it—maybe a tsunami would be more appropriate! Nevertheless, I have peace now. I possess all things now. I'm in love now. I sound like a new mother who has forgotten her birth pains upon viewing the prize. Paul says that he suffered the things he suffered because of his calling, which means it was ultimately for us.

> *Therefore do not be ashamed of the testimony of our Lord or of me His prisoner, but join with me in suffering for the gospel according to the power of God, who has saved us and called us with a holy calling, not according to our works, but according to His own purpose and grace which was granted us in Christ Jesus from all eternity, but has now been revealed by the appearing of our Savior Christ Jesus, who abolished death and brought life and immortality to light through the gospel, for which I was appointed a preacher and an apostle and a teacher. For this reason I also suffer these things, but I am not ashamed; for I know whom I have believed and I am convinced that He is able to guard what I have entrusted to Him until that day.*
>
> ~ 2 Timothy 1:8–12

What? Be a partaker of afflictions of the gospel by the power of God? Back to the point—it's better for me to write this now, and not when I have my brand new four-wheel drive truck sitting in the driveway of my beautiful new home! Because I can say these things now testifies that God is very real to me. My heart is to live in Him, *presently*. I love God's voice. I've had money and the American dream for a while, but it means nothing if I can no longer hear Him. He is the prize. And He knows my heart. I want to rely on the *now knowledge* of Him, being the prize, to stay with me through the next seasons of life.

CHAPTER 7

The Truth About Sin

I come from a place too good to be true to carnal thinking, a place where sin does not exist, a place of flying creatures and beautiful colors. It's where the River of Life flows. It's the place where Love Himself is seated on the throne. And the four living creatures circle the throne where Love Himself sits, and they say "holy, holy, holy"—nonstop, because they are beholding Him who sits on the throne in His glory. The twenty-four elders fall to their faces and lay their crowns before Love Himself. That is the place I live in my heart. I am in this earth but I am not of it.

The truth is, I don't really like to talk or think about sin. In fact, I exercise a lot of faith reckoning myself and am dead to it because it's no longer I that live, but Christ that lives in me. Sin is now irrelevant because Jesus destroyed the law of sin and death on the cross. Sin is no longer the issue. The issue now is whether or not we exercise our faith to live in

Christ or not, because that point of fact is the only justification there is to possess. I was crucified with Jesus, buried with Him, and resurrected with Him. I no longer look at myself after the flesh, and I do not want to look at anyone else after the flesh. I want to look at what is not as though it is, so that it shall be. However, when we live in Love Himself, we will produce the fruit of love. We will not sin, in the sense of disobedience, and love fulfills the law.

So let's talk about sin. Let's see, there are the sins we hate, and there are the sins we love. There are sins we love to hate, and there are sins we hate that we love! There are socially accepted sins, and socially rejected sins. There are sins that make you feel cool, and sins that break all the rules. There are sins that are not seen, and sins that are seen. There are sins that seem not so bad, and sins that seem horrendous. Some sin scares us; other sins entertain us. Some sin knows our first name and where we live. Some sins wink at us, while other sins abuse us. There are sins that are sin to one, and not to another. There is sin everywhere—at work, school, church, home, the ball field, television, radio, news, monasteries, ministry schools, in our nation's capital, each other, our preacher, our wives, our children, ourselves, etc.

The Apostle John says any man who says he doesn't have sin is sinning. So what is it? What does it do? Where did it come from? Was it something I caught? Was it something I ate? Is there a cure? Is it hereditary? Is it a genetic condition? Will I break out with something? Is it going to hurt? Is it sexually transmitted? Can I be arrested for it? Can I die from it?

Well, that gives us a lot to talk about, doesn't it? It is something we are all guilty of and have to acknowledge, or we sin again. The origin of sin was in the Garden of Eden, when Adam disobeyed God. Disobedience was released through the one who had authority of the earth. Therefore sin, or disobedience, was established by rite of passage through Adam. The seed of sin began to reproduce after itself, in various ways, and has plagued every generation since. And thanks to the lust of the eyes, the lust of the flesh, and the pride of life, we love the forbidden fruit. Scripture says we all have fallen short of the glory of God (Romans 3:23). So if this is true, when we look at each other, we are left only to be suspicious and wary. If all have sinned, then how can we ever trust each other again? I mean, if you did it once, you'll do it again, right?

THE SAME CONDITION OF SIN THAT WE ARE IN

Our natural instinct is to find those to hang around who share in the same condition of sin that we are in. For instance, if you are a thief, you probably feel better in the company of thieves. If you are an adulterer, you hang out with other adulterers. If you are a gossip, you probably hang out with someone who likes listening to it. If you walk with a religious spirit, you probably hang out with other ministers who have that same religious spirit. If you are rebellious, you like other rebellious-natured people. Birds of a feather flock together. We tend to congregate with our own. That's kind of spooky—that's how a lot of churches are formed!

What's funny and sad about this picture is that these same ones are pointing at one another's sin, as if they are an anomaly. We are fifty pounds overweight and pointing at homosexuals, as if we ourselves are excused for gluttony. We gossip about the drunk who lives in our neighborhood. We tell our neighbor's wife, while we lay beside her, how our wives are mean and unloving! We want to murder child molesters yet sleep with prostitutes. We judge the poor while we rob people blind, all in the name of our own sense of righteousness. We think we can isolate and eradicate some individuals while we vindicate ourselves. But that is not the righteous judgment of God. The righteous judgment of God is that all men have fallen short of the glory of God. Any man who says differently is a liar, and the truth is not in him. So, what happens when we sin?

But each one is tempted when he is carried away and enticed by his own lust. Then when lust has conceived, it gives birth to sin; and sin is accomplished, it brings forth death.

~ James 1:14–15

James clearly states sin brings forth death. It is the punishment of sin. Death can also be measured a number of different ways. For instance, if you steal, get caught, and are prosecuted, then you may get probation or go to prison for a season. So, the stigma of your sin may remain, and you might experience a level of death that follows you wherever you go. You may arouse suspicion; you might not be able to find good employment. Your wife may have left you while you were in jail. All of these things are ripple effects of death in certain ways and areas of your life. All of us have experienced those kinds of ripple effects in our own lives in some way or another.

Notice, in the Scripture, it says when lust has conceived, it gives birth to what ultimately becomes death. In other words, we become pregnant with death. That's not a pretty thought, is it? It kind of reminds me of the horror movie *Rosemary's Baby*. It is true: if we sleep with the Devil, we will bear his children! Likewise, if we commune with the spirit of God, and His word is planted in our hearts, we become pregnant with life, and we give birth to the life of God. That is when Heaven invades earth!

Another interesting nuance about that Scripture is that we are led away by our own desires. If another person has a desire that we don't have, that makes their sin seem worse to us. For example, if you are a man's man, you may have a little more sympathy and understanding for an adulterer than you would a homosexual. We seem to understand better how a person can get caught up in that sin condition than we do a desire that may be foreign to us. We tend to wink our eyes at what we can relate to, and justify our hatred of what we do not understand. We become Pharisees at heart, and it's causing almost irreparable damage to the witness of the church. So, people who have desires that are not common to ours have nowhere to go if they want help. They sure can't confess their temptations to sin to their brothers, because they will be ostracized and cursed by our mindsets against them. Jesus went about delivering, healing, and loving the most offensive and ostracized people of His culture. We tend to be angry at those people, and we do not realize that we were anointed to set them free.

DEATH GETS ITS STING FROM SIN

Death gets its sting from sin. Sin gets its strength from the law. The new creature in us gets its strength from the grace extended to us. Grace gets its strength from Love Himself.

The sting of death is sin, and the power of sin is the law...

~ 1 Corinthians 15:56

If this is the case, that sin gets its power from the law, then what will the accuser of the brethren use to accuse Christians with? The law! He can't accuse us any other way. He has to show us where we are not living up to the law. That is the only way he can bring us into the condemnation of sin-consciousness. That's why knowing what sin is doesn't give us any power to overcome it. Knowing what grace is through our revelation of Christ is the power that renders sin ineffective. Sin-consciousness gets its power from the law. Therefore, when the revelation of grace comes, sin-consciousness no longer has its platform of strength in us. We are saved by grace—not by our works of the law, but by His work on the cross. There would be no reason to exalt Jesus's victory on the cross if this didn't happen. So grace undermines, through the wisdom of God, the strength of sin in us.

Jesus destroyed the law of sin and death. The Ten Commandments are no longer a law to us, but are now the attributes of those who live in Christ. If you live in Christ, you no longer want to murder, steal, covet, or serve any other gods. When we choose Love Himself, we become the slave of that to which we obey. When we choose to be enslaved, by His love, He makes us a royal priesthood and looks at us as His own sons and daughters. When we choose to obey any other freedoms, we become enslaved to those things, and our slave master is not very kind!

Do you not know that when you present yourselves to someone as slaves for obedience, you are the slaves of the one whom you obey, either of sin resulting in death, or of obedience resulting in righteousness?

~ Romans 6:16

God knew all this existed. Because He so loved homosexuals, child molesters, evil dictators, Islamic extremists, murderers, drug-dealers, sexual perverts, prostitutes, tax collectors, satanic worshippers, liars, thieves, preachers, apostles, presidents, governors, lawyers, whoremongers, judges, nuns, abortion doctors, you, and your worst enemy, He gave His only begotten Son, that whosoever believed in Him would not perish, but have everlasting life. When John 3:16 says that, "God so loved the world," that is who He was talking about. I can feel your offense. I felt some offense writing it. It's because we hate what some of those people represent and do to others. I understand that. The fact remains that God calls us while we are yet sinners. There is no sin that occurs that doesn't produce death. Scripture says if you break one part of the law, it is as if you've broken every law (James 2:10).

GOD STILL LOVES THEM

Really, as hard as it may be to digest, without Christ, we are no different from the worst when it comes to the righteous standard of the law. Another factor that disturbs us when we read something like that is the fact that we want justice! We want people to pay for what they have done. We don't want evil people to get away with anything, especially those kinds of things. I spent most of my vocational life in law enforcement, and I have seen the ravages of sin. What God wants us to do is extend the same grace to others that we want extended to ourselves. Now, if I'm working as a deputy sheriff and I arrest a child molester, I will tell him about Christ on his way to jail. When someone commits an offense that injures or abuses others, they have to be stopped. Romans 13 says that the authorities are God's ministers of wrath for such as that. So I'm all about stopping evildoers; I just don't ever want to lose sight of the fact that, in spite of someone's atrocious behavior, God still loves them and wants them to turn their hearts to Him. God's justice is to see one of those sin types I just mentioned to be changed from that darkness and transformed by His glorious light. Their mission field will be those who know them, who are bound by the same things. Now that's justice!

Once, when I was a deputy, we had a murder occur in our county. The victim was a three-year-old child. I had to go inside the trailer where the murder occurred to retrieve an item for a detective who was in charge of the case. The man who killed the child was babysitting, and the child was misbehaving. He took the child and put him upside down in a kitchen trash can. The child suffocated. While I was in the little boy's room, I was looking at the toys on the floor that he would have been playing with last. I looked at his little bed where he slept and saw how he had moved his covers when he got up from his nap. All of a sudden, I was filled with rage; I wanted to kill the man who did this. I was so disturbed by what took place that I threw up. I was weeping, and I wanted to hurt him.

An unexpected yet remarkable thing happened. A couple of weeks later, I had to go to our state mental institution to pick up the offender from his mental diagnostic evaluation. I did not want to see this man; however, I had the job to pick him up. As I was on my way up there, I felt the Holy Spirit tell me to tell him about Jesus. What? I did not want this guy to know about Jesus. But the Lord was relentless, and somehow between Jesup and Milledgeville, God softened my heart.

After I picked him up, on our way back, the Lord just poured through me. I felt such a presence on me that I was amazed. I felt such an unreasonable love for this young man. I saw the Lord come upon this guy. I asked him if he wanted to receive Jesus, and he said yes. We prayed and he received Jesus. He wept and wept. My heart was so broken for this guy. Yes, the same one I wanted to put out of his misery. I believe he received Jesus that day, but three weeks later he hung himself in our jail. I hope and I believe he's with Jesus.

Somehow, we think, "I can understand God loving me, but not those kind of people." What we forget is that *we* were those kind of people. You might say, "I never did anything like that!" Well, let's see. Have you ever stolen anyone's joy with a bad attitude? If you did, that makes you a thief. Have you ever looked at anyone with lust? If you have, that makes you an adulterer. Have you ever hated your brother? If you have, according to Jesus, that makes you a murderer. Have you ever committed any sin? If you say you haven't, then what does that make you?

What God did was send Jesus, who became sin for us, who by His death on the cross destroyed sin and death. Now everyone who chooses to follow Jesus and live for Him can appropriate that life in exchange for their own. It's called beauty for ashes. They no longer have any excuses not to follow after Love Himself. We are no longer judged by the law, but by our faith in Jesus, and we are changed from the inside out. Our excuses were nailed to the cross. God has dealt with our sin. What's left is the *outgoing residual* of what was. Now, we set our minds on Christ and reckon ourselves dead to sin because now we live in Christ, and there is no sin in Him!

But I say, walk by the Spirit, and you will not carry out the desire of the flesh.

~ Galatians 5:16

Now those who belong to Christ have crucified the flesh with its passions and desires.

~ Galatians 5:24

Therefore if anyone is in Christ, he is a new creature; the old things passed away; behold, new things have come. Now all these things are from God, who reconciled us to Himself through Christ and gave us the ministry of reconciliation, namely, that God was in Christ reconciling the world to Himself, **not counting their trespasses against them***, and He has committed to us the word of reconciliation.*

~ 2 Corinthians 5:17–19 (emphasis added)

I would expect that most of us heard these Scriptures for the first time when we were born again. These are some of the Scriptures that help a person get established in their new walk and see what God has done for them. We love the grace that was extended to us, but we tend to want others to receive the justice of the law. The reason I haven't differentiated between the world and the church on this subject is because we do the same things. Often we look just like the world, and we justify it with a theology of man that's not fit and should be flushed down a toilet. We become the accuser of the brethren in a sense. We try to remove the speck from our brother's eye when we have a plank hanging out of our own (Matthew 7:3). If we really were blind, we would have no sin, but because we say we see, our sin remains (John 9:41). If you really want to ignite the wrath of God, keep on condemning something in others that His Son destroyed on the cross two thousand years ago.

This one thing I do know: if we are offended so much by any person with a particular sin, we will not be able to minister Jesus to them. For example, if I am so offended by homosexuals, so much that I hate them, I cannot minister the love of God to them. So many are blinded by hate, unforgiveness, and a spirit of self-righteousness in their own lives. The sins that bother us the most are usually the ones others struggle with.

Love and hate cannot live in the same house. You would literally be divided against yourself, and you would eventually fall if you do not deal with your offense. It is true that we can love and hate. For example, I should love righteousness but hate sin. However, I should not love sin and hate sin, or love righteousness and hate righteousness. It is at that point where we would be divided. We can love the sinner while hating the sin that has imprisoned them. I've heard some who call themselves Christians say they wished homosexuals were all dead. Jesus paid such a horrific price for *all* of us; how can we withhold His love from *any*? I'm not saying that, if someone is trying to break into your home, you should just let them in to possibly harm your family so you can minister the love of God to them. I'm not saying that. You do what you have to do to protect yourself and your family; then, if they are conscious, you can minister the love of God to them!

THE GOD WE SERVE DIED FOR ALL

Here is the point of all this: if we don't love the unlovable, then who will? If we don't see the treasure in a person that God put in them, then who will? If we don't lay down our political correctness, our idols of convenience, and our mindfulness of the thoughts of men, then who will? We have to choose who we are going to serve, because the God we serve died for all.

If you saw a homosexual or a child molester who was sick and in pain, would you desire that he be made whole? Would your great love well up inside and overflow toward him? Would you pray for his healing? If you did and they were healed, right there on the spot, do you think God would have their full attention? Do you think they might sense the need to repent of their ways? It is the goodness of God that leads men to repentance.

> *Or do you think lightly of the riches of His kindness and tolerance and patience, not knowing that* **the kindness of God leads you to repentance?**
>
> ~ Romans 2:4 (emphasis added)

To my knowledge, not one person was born again when Jesus healed them. They were either Jews or Gentiles. Not one person who received deliverance was born again when they were delivered. Peter wasn't born again when he walked on water. When Jesus was hanging on the cross, He said, *"Father, forgive them; for they do not know what they are doing"* (Luke 23:34). He did not say, "Father, forgive them when they are born again." He forgave all mankind, and when He drew His last breath, He said, *"It is finished!"* (John 19:30). He forgave us when we were yet sinners. So, now, the Father doesn't look at our sin; He looks at whether or not we choose the grace He extended to us through His Son's work on the cross. Whether that comes in the form of our offer to pray for someone's healing or share the Gospel, if they receive the grace He is extending to them, they receive Him. We either make the choice for Love Himself, and bear the fruit of that choice, or we reject Him and live in the way of our own choosing, and bear that fruit. Jesus said it best:

"He who receives you receives Me, and he who receives Me receives Him who sent Me."

~ Matthew 10:40

I saw a Christian documentary where Heidi Baker was walking through a town in a Muslim country. She had a Christian interpreter who I believe was a pastor. She saw a Muslim woman who was in need of healing. She wanted the interpreter to tell the woman what she was saying. She was trying to tell the woman of Jesus's love for her and wanted to pray for her healing, but the interpreter refused to interpret for her because the woman was Muslim. It is that mentality the interpreter had which is binding the power of God to the world. Obviously, the interpreter wanted God's grace withheld because of the woman's faith, when God wanted to heal that woman and convert her from that faith. God's justice would have been that woman telling all her friends and family that she had been healed by Jesus. If it makes *you* feel any better, *she* would probably be killed for doing that, in her culture. If that thought does make you feel better, you need prayer for deliverance.

When it comes to certain moral offenders in our own country, we carry the same kinds of mindsets as the interpreter did. This *must* change.

FRUITS OF THE SPIRIT

The works we do when we choose Love Himself are called the fruits of the Spirit. These are: love, joy, peace, longsuffering, kindness, goodness, faithfulness, gentleness, and self-control, for against such there is no law (Galatians 5:22–23, paraphrased). The works we will do, if we don't choose the way of Love Himself, are called "works of the flesh." They are evident, and described as adultery, fornication, uncleanness, lewdness, idolatry, sorcery, hatred, contentions, jealousies, outbursts of wrath, selfish ambitions, dissentions, heresies, envy, murders, drunkenness, revelries, and the like. Those who practice these things will not inherit the Kingdom of God (Galatians 5:19–21).

The fruit we bear is the result of what we are grafted into. Where we are grafted into will be the result of receiving or rejecting Christ. We spend most of our time trying to pick off bad fruit, but if we don't lay the axe to the root, the fruit will come right back. We will know the tree by the fruit it bears. There is a big difference between a person who has been made righteous, who stumbles and occasionally sins, and a sinner who practices sin.

> *Even so consider yourselves to be dead indeed to sin, but alive to God in Christ Jesus.*
>
> *Therefore do not let sin reign in your mortal body so that you obey it in its lusts, and do not go on presenting the members of your body to sin as instruments of unrighteousness; but present yourselves to God as those alive from the dead, and your members as instruments of righteousness to God. For sin shall not be master over you, for **you are not under law but under grace.***
>
> ~ Romans 6:11–14 (emphasis added)

Last night, my wife Christy read a lot of this chapter you are reading. When we lay down in the bed, just before we went to sleep, she said something very profound. She said, "You know, lawyers study the law to be an advocate or a prosecutor for a person who is charged with a crime. Their only advocate is a man who determines what the law is, regarding their outcome." She said she had been reading the book of Job, and Job was saying, "I wish there was a mediator between me and God to plead my case" (Job 9:33, paraphrased). When she said that, it ignited my thinking; that is so true.

Men study the law to decide what's just and what's not just. That's what the scribes did in Jesus' day. If the law is all that can justify us, then there is nothing left for us but Hell itself, because Jesus said all have sinned. However, the Father no longer judges His children according to the law. He looks to see if a person is walking in the grace He extended to us, by faith in the work Jesus finished on the cross. We are saved by grace, through faith. If we live by faith in Christ, it is accounted to us as righteousness, sealed by the Holy Spirit. Jesus is now our advocate, who is with the Father and intercedes on our behalf. We're not judged according to the law, but grace! We are now free to do whatever we want; Jesus abolished the law of sin and death. All things are lawful. But Paul is clear that whatever we yield ourselves to, we are that one's slave whom we obey.

And through Him everyone who believes is freed from all things from which you could not be freed by the Law of Moses.

~ Acts 13:39

THE PRESENCE-PURPOSED LIFE

For sin shall not be master over you, for you are not under law but under grace.

~ Romans 6:14

For what the law could not do, weak as it was through the flesh, God did: sending his own Son in the likeness of sinful flesh and as an offering for sin, He condemned sin in the flesh…

~ Romans 8:3

THE THIEF

The thief does not come except to steal, and to kill, and to destroy. I have come that they may have life, and that they may have it more abundantly.

~ John 10:10

The ole thief—he usually never comes like you think he might. He's probably not going to tempt you with what offends you. For instance, if you saw a burglar walking around in your yard, you would probably lock your doors, call 911, and arm yourself with a weapon. You would be ready to fight. The enemy does impose himself sometimes, but usually it's another way. The burglar in your yard is an illustration you can understand, so here's another. Let's say you're a guy, and it's a supermodel in your yard. Uh-oh, are you being led away by your own desires? Why is this beautiful woman in my yard? You look out the window, and she smiles and winks at you. Maybe your wife's not home. You think, "What's the harm? I'll see what she wants." You find yourself unlocking your door. The next thing you know, you're backing her truck up to your door and helping her carry all your goods and possessions out of your house. She waves goodbye and she's off, never to be seen again, unless she thinks she can repeat the crime. That's how the devil steals our goods. He comes in a way that entices us to actually assist him in our own destruction. This method can look a hundred different ways, but here is the bottom line: we are left empty and hurt—even destroyed. He always hits us where we are weak.

When I went to the police academy years ago, they taught us that criminals usually need two components to commit a crime: motive and opportunity. For Christians, as well as unbelievers, the devil's motive is to kill, steal, and destroy. He wants to sow his lies to try to prohibit us from seeing Jesus. The opportunities he looks for are our areas of weakness. Wherever we are weak, that is what he seeks to exploit. Unfortunately, in the natural, the elderly and women are prime suspects for predators because of physical weakness and vulnerability. Predators seek an environment that they feel confident they can control. For Christians, concerning our spiritual walk, Satan usually presents bait to entice our desires, sort of like fishing. When you fish, you try different lures or jigs to see what the fish are biting. When you know what they are biting, you know how to catch them. So the fish symbol really is fitting for us. Once he knows what we are biting, we're already fried! When we live and move and have our being in the Spirit of God, we have to be lured away by forbidden fruit, which is Satan's bait.

Satan comes to steal our joy, our peace, our finances, our health, and our ability to produce the fruits of the Spirit. He wants us to doubt God. He wants us to blame God. He wants to steal our identities and credibility. He is proud of what he does. Every time one of us falls, he pats himself on the back, but that is the only comfort he will ever have, and it's only in a vapor of time. When we live in Christ effectively, he has nothing in common with us. When he sees us living and moving and having our being in Christ, he cannot find bait that will work.

Our determination to choose Love Himself is key. Scripture says in James 4:7, paraphrased, "Submit to God, resist the devil, and he will flee from you." We usually just hear, "Resist the devil, and he will flee." Remember the key: we must be submitted to having our being in Christ, and then our very lives will rebuke him! That's really all the press I want to give him in this book.

CHAPTER 8

The Hall of Justice

The Hall of Justice is the place where judgment is made. It's the place we are turned over to when we have broken the law. In the natural, that would be our court system. Coming from a law enforcement background, I saw the court system at work for many years. I saw the same offenders go through the system—from prosecution to incarceration—only to see them again. Law enforcement personnel call our court system "the revolving door." Over and over, the same people seem to get caught doing the same things they just got out of prison for. "Once a thief, always a thief" is a mentality that we seem to believe as a life principle. It does seem to be the rule, but it is not the truth. The problem with our system is not the law, the prosecution, or the crime. It's the heart condition of the offender, and the impotence of the law to change the heart condition.

Let's go to church. In our local assemblies, we often hear preachers holding up the letter of the law, with the indictment of naming particular sins that people are walking in. The people hear this and realize they are not measuring up to the law. Then we see the same people go to the altar over and over again for the same thing. They sincerely weep and repent, and then they get up again to start over anew. But is that it? Are they now fixed and ready to go? The answer is no, because without a revelation of Jesus, their heart condition is the same, and we will see the process repeat itself in their lives. Many will argue it was the revelation of Jesus that showed them their guilt. But I say it is the revelation of not measuring up to the law that makes you guilty. Our services have become too much like the court system. We know how to arrest, prosecute, and incarcerate, but we are impotent in changing the heart condition. The strength of sin comes from the law. When we see the upholding of the law as the answer to sin, we increase the power of sin in the person's life.

The sting of death is sin, and **the power of sin is the law***…*

~ 1 Corinthians 15:56 (emphasis added)

The court system and some churches are so impotent because there is only one thing that renders sin powerless. It is the revelation of Love Himself. The revelation of Jesus Christ and His grace towards us are the only things that can stop the revolving doors. When you truly see Jesus for who He is, you will know the grace that has been extended to you. Grace destroys the platform that empowers sin to stand. It's impossible to truly encounter God's grace without it weakening the strongholds of the enemy in our lives.

When Jesus destroyed the law of sin and death, everything that empowered sin was destroyed. The revelation of grace destroys sin-consciousness. Even if some contradictions remain in your life, they no longer have the power over you that they once had, and they are passing away. Sin can retain the power it once had only when we begin to listen to the accuser of the brethren again. The accuser of the brethren can come in many forms, but ultimately he comes from the lies perpetuated by the accuser himself. He is the father of lies, so even if he is not personally delivering the lie to you, he is the father of it.

Accusations can come through anyone or anything. You may be accused by your enemies, friends, preachers, yourself, your circumstances, failures, family, addictions, sin, or anything that would be contrary to who God says you are in Him. Those are the contradictions to the truth of who you are. You may in fact be an addict, but that's not the truth. If you are born again, you are more than a conqueror. You can no longer look at yourself after the flesh; you have to look at yourself after the spirit. You must look at others also after the spirit.

We are not who the contradictions say we are. Psalm 23:5 says that God prepares a table for us in the presence of our enemies, that He anoints our heads with oil and our cups run over. That is who God is to us and for us. Our enemies are any and all of the contradictions that say otherwise. God wants us to overflow presently, in spite of our current circumstances. We have to reckon ourselves dead to sin, contradictions, or any other circumstances in order to see Him clearly. We have to determine in our hearts to do that. It is a paradox that does not seem reasonable to natural thinking, but it is the way He has made for us.

Grace enables us. Grace justifies us. Grace purifies us. Grace keeps us. Grace changes us. Grace glorifies us. Grace is true. Jesus is Grace Himself! When you hear someone speak to a king, you will often hear them refer to the king as "Your Grace." Jesus is the King of Kings, His Grace Himself. If grace is the power of Love Himself, then it is certainly the wisdom of Love Himself. It is His wisdom to release grace to sinners. The throne room of grace is the only place where the justice of God is found for all who have ears to hear.

THE HEAVENLY COURT

Hear ye, hear ye, hear ye, the heavenly court of God is now in session, to change what cannot be changed, to uphold what cannot be upheld, to break what cannot be broken, to leave what cannot be left, to right what cannot be made right, to give liberty to those in chains. Who can do such a thing? Who can drink this cup? Who can eat this scroll? The Chief Justice, Love Himself, whom there is no law against, but is the Fulfillment and the Author of the law, Who sees what cannot be seen and loves those who cannot be loved, Who enables those who cannot stand, and redeems those who lay condemned? Where can this justice be found? Only in the throne room of Grace! Who can find such justice? Those who say, "I'm poor, miserable, blind, and naked." Those who say, "It's me in the need of prayer." Those who say, "I hunger and thirst for righteousness." Those who are desperate to bear His love, they will say, "Where are my accusers?" They will say, "I was blind but now I see." They will say, "I was naked, and He clothed me." They will say, "He visited me in my prison." They will say, "I was hungry and He gave me food to eat." They will say, "I was thirsty and He gave me drink." They will say, "He visited me when I was sick." They will say, "We heard Him speak from a whirlwind in the thorn tree." They will say, "I ate from His table in the presence of my enemies!" They will sing the songs of deliverance! They will walk on water! They will run on the walls of the enemy! They will lead captives out of prisons! They will love Me and keep my commandments! This court is adjourned!

Wow, I love those spontaneous words from the Lord! I hope the reader of this book is getting as blessed as the writer. God is so good. He loves us so much, that He reveals Himself to us. He is good. He is just.

When I was in law enforcement, we had to investigate incidents and automobile accidents. Sometimes while patrolling, we might witness a crime in progress. Regardless of what we were involved with, we had to write a report of the evidence we obtained, whether it was physical evidence or what we may have witnessed ourselves. We did this so our testimony in court would possess the details of what we witnessed. Sometimes the legal process could take months or even years for a case to go to trial. In some cases, you might be asked to recount your involvement from an incident twenty years ago.

Recently, I was contacted by an investigator for the district attorney's office. The investigator said that a death penalty case had been overturned in a murder conviction. This crime happened nineteen years ago. He needed me to recount the details of my involvement in the case. My first thought was, "Are you kidding me?" But one thing that all officers are trained to do is detail in their reports what their involvement was. It is for this purpose that we made detailed reports. I did tell the investigator what I could from memory, but asked him to retrieve the report I made at the time. Because I can swear to the testimony I wrote at the time. When you are being cross-examined by a defense attorney, you are trained to refer only to your report. You don't add to it, or withhold from it. You do not embellish it later. You just rely on the facts of your report. When you write it, you know you are writing what you may possibly have to swear to if the offender doesn't reach a plea bargain.

WE HAVE TO REMEMBER THE JESUS WE MET

When we as Christians are being cross-examined by the accuser, we have to swear by what we have seen with our eyes and heard with our ears. We have to refer back to what has been written in our hearts. We have to remember where He found us. What we were doing. We have to remember our first love. We have to remember the Jesus we met, and not the one we may see being portrayed. We must have an encounter with Jesus to testify to what we have seen by the Spirit. It is that testimony that overcomes our accuser. We overcome by the blood of the Lamb and the word of our testimony.

What was from the beginning, what we have heard, what we have seen with our eyes, what we have looked at and touched with our hands, concerning the Word of Life—and the life was manifested, and we have seen and testify and proclaim to you the eternal life, which was with the Father and was manifested to us—what we have seen and heard we proclaim to you also, so that you too may have fellowship with us; and indeed our fellowship is with the Father, and with His Son Jesus Christ. These things we write, so that your joy may be made complete.

This is the message we have heard from Him and announce to you, that God is Light and in Him there is no darkness at all. If we say that we have fellowship with Him and yet walk in the darkness, we lie and do not practice the truth; but if we walk in the Light as He is in the Light, we have fellowship with one another, and the blood of Jesus His Son cleanses us from all sin. If we say that we have no sin, we are deceiving ourselves and the truth is not in us. If we confess our sins, He is faithful and righteous to forgive us our sins and to cleanse us from all unrighteousness. If we say that we have not sinned, we make Him a liar, and His word is not in us.

~ 1 John 1:1–10

In the book of John, Jesus was in the temple teaching where one of the greatest accounts of His grace is recorded.

Early in the morning He came again into the temple, and all the people were coming to Him; and He sat down and began to teach them. The scribes and the Pharisees brought a woman caught in adultery, and having set her in the center of the court, they said to Him, "Teacher, this woman has been caught in adultery, in the very act. Now in the law Moses commanded us to stone such women; what then do You say?" They were saying this, testing Him, so that they might have grounds for accusing Him. But Jesus stooped down and with His finger wrote on the ground. But when they persisted in asking Him, He straightened up, and said to them, "He who is without sin among you, let him be the first to throw a stone at her." Again He stooped down and wrote on the ground. When they heard it, they began to go out one by one, beginning with the older ones, and He was left alone, and the woman, where she was, in the center of the court. Straightening up, Jesus said to her, "Woman, where are they? Did no one condemn you?" She said, "No one, Lord." And Jesus said, "I do not condemn you, either. Go From now on sin no more."

~ John 8:2–11

That is an incredible story. We love to see ourselves as the one Jesus released that kind of grace to. We should see ourselves in that position, but we should also want to see others receive the same grace released to them. It's hard for us to want our offenders let off the hook, but sooner or later we will have to learn to do just that. I know how hard that can be. I have spent a lifetime trying to learn this, and I am determined.

However, as much as I'm determined to forgive those who have hurt me, I don't like being tested in this. I'm just being honest. So take this moment to take a little exercise from this Scripture. I have already done this.

Picture a homosexual, caught in the act, being taken before Jesus like the woman caught in adultery. Or picture someone who may have hurt or abused you in her place. It may be a family member or a hardened criminal. It may be you. If you are like me, you may find that it's easier to accept the woman caught in adultery in that place, but not those we know personally. God wants us to forgive others so we will be released from the poison of their offense. However, that doesn't mean they will make Heaven just because we forgive them. A person who sets themselves up to be an offense to all that God is will not receive grace. That person is in pride. God has forgiven our sin, even those ignorant acts motivated by our pride. But if we do not relent in our pride, we are in real danger. God resists the proud. That's why He said, *"Many will say in that day, Lord, Lord."* And He will say, *"Depart from me I never knew you."* Then they will say, *"We prophesied in your name, we cast out devils in your name, and performed wonderful works"* (Matthew 7:21–23). What was the difference? *God is opposed to the proud, but gives grace to the humble* (James 4:6). God expects us to humble ourselves. The Holy Spirit will strive with them for a while, that they may come to their senses—but only for a set time.

Many times, Jesus would seem to be very hard against one group and gracious to another. He would rebuke one and heal another. If you don't understand this revelation that He resists the proud but gives grace to the humble, you could be tempted to think Jesus was unstable. But He was far from that. He sees what others cannot see, and He knows the hearts of others. God does not hold His tongue from prideful men unless He has a greater purpose to work, requiring His silence. Sometimes God's silence is deafening. That's why I love to hear His voice with my deaf ears and think His thoughts within my thick skull. That's not false humility—that's a fact. False humility is when we are proud of the great humility we walk in.

My brother, Bill, used to tell the story about this singer who sang in the church. When the service was over, the preacher went up to the singer and said, "That was some good singing." The singer gave a pious smile back and said, "It's just God, brother. It's just God." The preacher replied, "Well, now—it wasn't that good!" That's a funny story, but that is more than likely false humility, rooted in pride on the part of the singer.

There are two good questions that can be used as measuring sticks to help us determine whether or not we are in pride or humility.

Do you think you deserve the position you hold in life according to your own works, or greatness? If you are in ignorance or pride, then you would say yes. If you are walking in humility or false humility, you would say no.

Do you realize that every good and perfect gift that you have was given to you? If you are in ignorance or pride, you would say no. If you are walking in humility or false humility, you would say yes.

A person who walks in false humility is a wolf in sheep's clothing. They are infiltrators for their own agendas, or worse. They take advantage of gullible people and imprison them through manipulation and intimidation. In this state, they are of their father the devil, and they have learned the clichés of love but do not possess or understand the

Spirit of Love. In the days we are entering, if these people do not repent, they will become exposed and lay naked before all. We need the discernment of the Holy Ghost to know who's who.

We have to learn to hear His voice and to reflect His heart to all men specifically as He would lead, according to the grace that is working in us. He is the voice of justice!

CHAPTER 9

You

'When I was going through the worst season of my life, many people saw many things. To the world, I looked like a mess or failure. To the religious zealot, I looked like I was deceived, perhaps an abomination or an infidel. To my friends, I was a shell of what I once was, a walking contradiction. And I felt like I was all of those things. I remember the Trent Reznor song called, "Hurt," that Johnny Cash did on one of his final albums. I related to that song, because I believed that, if someone was around me long enough, I would eventually hurt them. But even in all these things, God saw something that no one else could see. When I and everyone else were seeing these negative things, God saw a book—not just this book you're reading, but He saw *me*, as a book that was being written by Him. Scripture says that He is the *author* and finisher of our faith. He saw a book whose pages contained the Bread of Life, whose pages would contain healing and direction, with chapters containing His heart, written by His hand, and not by the hands of men. He even saw unwritten pages, yet to come, with unique thought processes and perceptions that would undo the powers of darkness in others. So, the point of all this is to get to the subject matter of this section—you.

I didn't mean to put you on the spot. So, let's take this slowly. Who are you? What does the world see when it sees you? What does the church, as you know it, see when it sees you? What do your friends see when they see you? What does your family see? What do you see, when you look at yourself? What does God think about you? What is success to you? What's important to you? What are you afraid of? What or who do you believe in?

It's important to ponder these questions because your answers to them reveal your perception of yourself. Answering these questions determines what is influencing your self-perception. How you see yourself is crucial and foundational to your success. What I'm saying is not some positive thinking power mode that you will to do by your own ability. That kind of thinking is rooted in humanistic pride. Some people even use Scripture in the same manner. When our perception is distorted, then everything we see is in a distorted state of being, whether we are aware of that fact or not. In Titus 1:15, Paul writes:

> *To the pure, all things are pure; but to those who are defiled and unbelieving, nothing is pure, but both their mind and their conscience are defiled.*

If all of your answers to these questions reflect the beauty and glory of God, then that's awesome—go and sin no more! Be blessed. But if you didn't like what you were seeing and feeling, I have good news for you! Thanks be to God, He sees you in a much greater place than you may be able to see yourself in at the moment. And the future God has for you is not established in your distorted vision. Your present and your future is established by how God sees you *now*. When we see Jesus, and we *experience* how He sees us, we are empowered and enabled by His grace towards us. At that point, we have faith in God, and how we perceive things shifts from the old nature into the new. Now, when you see yourself, you can act accordingly to how you were created. Then you will see yourself and others with a pureness of heart. He sees you in your future presently.

HE SEES THE FINISHED WORK IN YOU

I heard Graham Cooke say it this way, "He loves you as you are now, and He loves the new emerging you." When God sees you, it's not your past that He's looking at. God deals with you presently from His future perspective of you, and you're drawn into your future. He sees the finished work in you. That is the faith of God toward you and working in you. Because He has faith to finish what He has started in you, His grace is released toward you right now.

When you live in Christ, God is not offended by your shortcomings or your failures. He is not surprised by them, either. He knew you would be dealing with these things when He called you to Himself. He's not in Heaven telling the angels, "What? Oh my goodness, I can't believe what he just did." No, He saw that seed in you, that would produce that thing you did, long before you ever saw it manifest. God is not dealing with your sin anymore because He *has already* dealt with sin. When Jesus was crucified, the demonic forces of hell made their final assault against Him. He took all your sin upon Himself and became sin. Jesus also experienced all of the Father's anger and wrath toward your sin, so much so that He knew the Father momentarily turned His face from Him. Jesus asked, *"Why have you forsaken Me?"* (Matthew 27:46). So, your sin, God's anger towards your sin, the curse of the law against your sin, and the power of darkness against your sin, were all nailed to the cross! How does God deal with you now?

God now deals with you according to the righteous identity you have in Him because of your choice to believe in Jesus—who made the ultimate sacrifice. You see Him as the Lamb slain for the appeasement of your sin. You are a new creature who was made righteous because of the choice you made to follow Him (Romans 5:19). All of your sin is under the blood of Christ, so He is not looking to crucify you. You were made righteous by Jesus the moment you received Him. So you don't do good works so that you will be made righteous, you do good works because you are righteous! He crucified those things about you that still try to imprison you. When you identify yourself with your old nature, your perception of who you are becomes distorted. It's when you live from this distorted perception of yourself that you produce bitter fruit. So what is the answer? Proverbs 29:18 (ESV) says:

> *Where there is no prophetic vision the people cast off restraint, but blessed is he who keeps the law.*

This is an Old Testament proverb, and we are no longer under the law of Moses, but the law of Christ. However, being that Christ fulfilled the law, the truth of this Scripture remains. The word *vision* in the Hebrew was translated from the word *chazon*, which means a *mental sight*, that is, a *dream, revelation,* or *oracle*. An *oracle* is someone who speaks the revealed heart of God. Prophets can be called oracles. A *revelation* is an epiphany of God's heart. A *mental sight,* or a *dream,* is a vision of God's heart. So, when the word *vision* is used in this Scripture, it is talking about a *now* vision or *revelation* of Jesus. It's not talking about a long-term mission plan or vision statement for your life; it's talking about a continual vision or living revelation of God's heart toward you presently. Now, when you speak, you speak from the living waters you are living in. That is who you are! When you live in this place, you have the permission of ownership, because you are His. It's impossible not to bear good fruit.

The enemy knows how dangerous you are in this place, so he spends all of his energy trying to deceive and distort your vision. The word *perish* used in this Scripture comes from the word *para*. Some of its meanings are *to go back, to make naked,* and *to set at naught*. *To go back* obviously would be to go back to our old way of thinking. *To make naked* is what happened to Adam and Eve's perception when they ate from the forbidden tree. *To be set at naught* is to be brought to nothing. Have you ever felt like you've been brought to nothing? Well, when you live in Christ, all the news is good.

CONTEND FOR HIS PRESENCE

In the encounter I had on June 1, 2010, one of the things the Lord told me was to contend for His presence. When we contend for His presence, we are contending for a *now revelation* of Christ. When we experience

Jesus in His glory, we are changed. It's impossible for anything else to happen. You cannot encounter the manifest presence of Jesus without being changed. To abide in His presence is to abide in the vine. When you abide in the vine, He manifests Himself to you.

There are many ways to contend for His presence: through reading the Scripture, worship, prayer, meditation of His word, fellowship with other believers, anointed messages, etc. But when He is revealed, we need to stop, look, and listen. Bob Jones released a prophetic word about "stop, look, and listen." That's the rule you teach your children to do before they cross the road. That is definitely a rule that applies to following Jesus.

You have a unique destiny to fulfill. An assignment no one else can accomplish. When God sees you, He may hear a song yet to be played with soothing melodies, never before heard, that expresses His heart. That's what God sees. When God sees you, He may see a painting with many textures and colors that reveal His beauty like nothing ever seen by man before that moment—your moment. When God sees you, He may see a hero who makes a stand when injustice raises its ugly head. It is the heart of the Lion of Judah Himself that brings fear and impotence to the enemy! That's what God sees when He sees you. That's the kind of life God wants for you. That's the success He wants you to have: all the fulfillment and joy of heaven, here on earth.

God sees you individually as the church, a safe place. He sees you as the environment that someone can walk into and receive peace, shelter from the storm, grace, healing, truth, love, and empowerment: a place of forgiveness, a place where darkness is displaced by the light of His grace, a place where demonic forces have no power or influence. That's how God sees you.

How do you get to this place? Determine in your heart to get to Jesus. He rewards those who diligently seek Him. Ask and it shall be given to you, seek and you will find, knock and the door will be open to you. Jesus will in no way leave the door closed if you seek to get in! God is good, and He says, *"Come to Me, all who are weary and heavy-laden, and I will give you rest. For My yoke is easy and My burden is light"* (Matthew 11:28, 30).

Jesus will get you through the storms of life. These things are temporary moments that exist in a vapor of time.

CHAPTER 10

Success

Success—it's what everyone hopes for. It's what everyone shoots for. We work hard for it. We study for it, we train for it, we build for it, we fight for it! We love it. We need it, and we want it. Some people will do anything they can to get it. And all people would agree that it is the goal of life, but what is it? What is success? Is it financial freedom? Is it being healthy? Is it a great job? Is it a state of intellectual achievement? Is it being dealt a good hand in a poker game? Is it being lucky? Is it not going to hell when it's all said and done? Is it finding your soul mate? Is it having a family? Success is many things to many people. In the United States, we call success fulfilling the American dream. In many city slums across the globe, finding a sturdy box to sleep in that night might be success. To a drug addict, finding his next fix may seem like success. To a prostitute, not getting AIDS might seem like success. Success is many

THE PRESENCE-PURPOSED LIFE

things to many people. So, what is success for a Christian? What does it mean to be successful in the eyes of our Creator?

To this world's system, being a success would be to achieve higher learning through education, have a well-paying job that fulfills a sense of purpose, be a homeowner and maybe give back to the community, and join civic organizations and be a pillar of your community. All this sounds nice, and it's ok to do these things, but I still believe success is much more than this. Some people will never be able to accomplish what I just described, but I believe everyone can achieve success. I believe stepping into success can happen immediately. Not everyone will call it success, but you will experience it, regardless of what others see.

Most people, even in the secular world, want to feel free. They want freedom: financial freedom, freedom from guilt, freedom from fear, freedom to do as they please, etc. Some people will kill for it; some people will die for it. Some people will steal for it; some people will lie for it. Some people will do anything imaginable to have it. They may even sell their soul for it. Some will go to Hell for it.

On CNN, I recently heard a commentator say, "Knowledge is the new power." I believe this to be true, but I don't believe it's from the same tree that I'm thinking of. People want power because they can use that power to achieve freedom. People are hungry for power because they are starving for freedom. People want independence from anything that restricts their sense of freedom. Therefore, this kind of freedom is not truly freedom—it's an idol, to which the whole world seems enslaved. Remember what Paul said:

Do you not know that when you present yourselves to someone as slaves for obedience, you are the slaves of the one whom you obey, either of sin resulting in death, or of obedience resulting in righteousness?

~ Romans 6:16

So, freedom is no longer freedom because we as a people have enslaved ourselves to the pursuit of freedom. Convenience is a close relative that also has become an idol which we love to worship. We withhold our love when it doesn't feel convenient to us. We want what we want when we want it. We have spoiled ourselves in the name of freedom and convenience.

All too often, you hear the principles of the Gospel preached so that people feel that they possess the power to achieve the American dream. Believe me, I absolutely believe that God wants us to prosper, as our soul prospers, and be in health. That's scriptural, but that's not the defining sign that determines whether a person is successful or not. If it is, then don't read anything Paul wrote, because he didn't look successful while chained in prison. Stephen didn't look successful when he was being stoned. Corrie Ten Boom didn't look successful when she was in a Nazi concentration camp. Martin Luther King, Jr., didn't look successful when he was lying in a pool of his own blood after being shot for sharing a dream God gave him. Missionaries going to Africa, living in the jungle with natives to share the love of God, don't look like the American dream, but ask yourself, were they successful?

So if power, freedom, and convenience are not the prize, then what is? Jesus said that His Kingdom was not of this world. When Jesus walked the earth, He lived and functioned from His Kingdom. He was in the world but not of it. Scripture says that, when we are born again, we are in this world but not of it. So, what is success? I can tell you what it is *not*. It is not of this world, nor is it mindful of the things of men, as men perceive. It is mindful of the things of God, and God is mindful of men as He perceives.

SUCCESS IS EATING FROM THE TREE OF LIFE

To be successful is to have the mind of Christ. To be successful is to live and move and have my being in Him, to be transformed into the likeness and image of Christ, to obey His voice, to commune with Him. To be successful is to behold Him in his glory. Success is seeing Christ revealed as the prize of life. Success is righteousness, peace, and joy in the Holy Ghost. Success is when it's no longer I that lives, but Christ that lives in me. Success is when I only say what I hear Him saying, and I only do what I see Him doing. Success is when I love God with all my heart, strength, soul, and mind. Success is when I have the capacity to love others. Success is when I'm not offended because of Him. Success is when I'm not offended because of you. Success is when you're not offended because of me. Success is doing the will of Him who sent me. Success is to be the recipient of His grace. Success is being born again.

Success is eating from the Tree of Life. Success is healing the sick, casting out devils, giving sight to the blind. Success is being blessed by the hand of God and walking in that favor. Success is not quitting. Success is seeing things that are not as though they are, so that they shall be. Success is living in that faith now. Success is being forgiven and forgiving others. Success is being able to boldly go into the throne room of grace in time of need. Success is being like the throne room of grace for others in their times of need. Success is when we see that Jesus is the prize and fulfillment of all things. He is the prize! He fulfills the longings or our hearts. He gives us purpose, rest, and the right to freedom by His righteousness. He gives us dignity. He gives us liberty. He gives us justice! Success is finding our ownership of who we are in Christ, and our food is to do His will.

PURPOSED TO LIVE IN HIS PRESENCE

We are successful the moment we start this journey. Does this get under your skin? I hope it gets under your skin and into your heart! There is no greater success to achieve than to fulfill your destiny in Christ. You were created for this moment in time. There is no greater destiny than to achieve and complete your calling in Christ, and you were called to dwell in Him. You were called to live and move and have your being in Him. You were purposed to live in His presence.

There are a lot of people who look successful, even according to a lot of doctrines and traditions of men being taught from pulpits. However, many of these people never fulfill the destiny that God planned for them. If this doesn't look or feel like what you were hoping for, my hope is that you will not walk away sad. My hope is that, if these things are not exciting to you, then you can use this as a measuring stick of how your vision may have declined, that you would get eye salve from Jesus that will open your eyes to remember your first love, that moment when the knowledge and encounter of Him was enough, and your soul found peace and newness of life. If you know this is what you need, take this time and ask for it. He will in no way withhold this from you.

POINTING YOU TOWARD CHRIST

You have done well; you have chosen Love Himself. All of us have a path of obedience that we must follow. You cannot follow the path alone, though—you must follow the leading of the Holy Spirit. The Holy Spirit: He is our comforter. He empowers us from on high. You can trust Him explicitly. He will always point you to Christ. He will guide you to every destination ordained for you. He will lead you to every door that leads you to your destiny. If you stay on your path that God lays out for you, then you will have authority everywhere you walk. When you step off of the path God has designed for you, you step out of your authority. Your path of obedience and your authority in Christ are married to each other. When you desire to get back on your path, the Holy Spirit will lead you back there. When you return to your path, you return to your authority.

You cannot be distracted by another person's path, or you will lose sight of your own path. You should not covet or compare another one's path to yours, either. That will cause a decrease in vision. When you follow the Holy Spirit, you are immediately on the path God called you to walk. You may share a path with another from time to time, but even then, it must be your path at that moment. You must keep communion with Him, and as you walk, then you will have the revealed vision of Him. Your path is made for you, designed to take you to the places that you specifically need in order to be equipped to fulfill your calling. That's why it is so important that you focus on *your path* of obedience. God knows what you need when you need it to get to the next level. He is the master of stewardship.

Sometimes, you may feel that you are off of your path when the world seems to turn upside down on you. When you are experiencing everything but His goodness, that doesn't necessarily mean you are off your path. The Holy Spirit may have led you straight to this place to deal with your character and integrity—maybe even to show you that you don't have any, and therefore we're going to camp here awhile! We are developing, just like a photo being processed from film in a darkroom. As we develop, we continue on the path with the increase from what each season brings.

Your path is where you find your life, but it is also where you lose your life. It is your inheritance and your cross. What does that look like? It's the very thing that was designed for you from the beginning. It is the pressure that creates the diamond. It mines out the gold. It purifies you like gold and silver. It is the path of process and change. It is the paradox that contains the contradiction of everything you are, that separates the wheat from the chaff on the threshing floor. It is the stigma of the wisdom of this age. It is the process that signs and wonders follow. It is where miracles happen, where the knowledge of God's goodness and love are found and deepened. It is the path of life, and few find it. It's something that has to be embraced. It is good news if you have eyes to see. Most Christians want the benefits, but not the inconvenience. If you follow God, you will not be politically correct. You may not even be correct to the traditions and doctrines of men, but you will be a breath of fresh air to a sick and dying world! You may be viewed as someone who is wasting your life.

SHE CAME WASTING

A friend of mine, Trevor Haug, wrote a song called "She Came Wasting." It's the story of the woman with the alabaster box that contained a very expensive ointment. She poured it on Jesus's head as He reclined. When this happened, His own disciples became indignant, for that ointment could have been sold and the money given to the poor. Jesus told them what she did was a good thing. The world will see you as wasting your life, because they do not understand this vapor of time we are living in. Jesus loves extravagant expressions of our love. She came wasting. The wisdom of this age and religious spirits see waste. God sees much Love.

Somehow, in our western culture, we seem to think that God is not requiring us to lay down our lives for His. I remember a funny story my brother Parker used to tell. He said he was witnessing to a guy about Jesus, and the guy said, "Yeah, I believe in Him, but I don't think He should try to run your life!" That was so funny to me on the one hand, but sad on the other because that is what a lot of Christians believe.

In some countries and cultures, you put your life at risk the moment you make a profession of faith in Christ. When some people receive Jesus, they have to embrace a possible death sentence from that moment on. When I hear these things, I'm blown away at the courage they have—brand-new believers stepping into a satanic gauntlet of persecution on day one. How would you like to carry that cross? We fall asleep in church over here when the word is being preached, and they would risk their lives to have what puts us to sleep. We need a revelation of Christ. We must contend for His presence.

Jesus said He only did what He saw his Father do, and He only said what He heard His Father say. That was the life He said He lived. If that's true, then following the Holy Spirit led Him straight to the cross. Many might say, "Well, that was Jesus, and that was His purpose." I agree with that. So, then, let's take Paul. Paul said, "It's no longer I that lives, but Christ that lives in me. The life I now live is Christ" (Galatians 2:20, paraphrased). If that's true, then I am left to believe that the Holy Spirit led him to imprisonment and ultimately to be beheaded. You might say "Well, he was an apostle!" Okay, then, let's take Stephen. He wasn't Christ or an apostle. But he boldly spoke the living word and was accused of blaspheming Moses and God by those men from a certain synagogue, and they stoned him to death for it. How about Martin Luther King Jr.'s dream—was that from God or men? If it was from God, his dream cost him his life. *Oh my gosh, don't preach like that…you'll ruin my conference!* Listen to these words that were written and put to music by the late Keith Green:

The world is sleeping in the dark
that the Church just can't fight,
'cause it's asleep in the light.
How can you be so dead,
when you've been so well fed?
Jesus rose from the grave.
And you! You can't even get out of bed!

I don't want to sound fatalistic, nor do I want or feel the need to prove anything. I hope that, if I was faced with such a thing, I could stand for Christ no matter what. But when we were born, we were born into a war that is literally life and death. People are dying all the time for following

Jesus, and I don't think He sees any failures among them. This life is a vapor, and there is ground to take.

For we who live are constantly being delivered over to death for Jesus' sake, so that the life of Jesus also may be manifested in our mortal flesh.

~ 2 Corinthians 4:11

For to me, to live is Christ and to die is gain.

~ Philippians 1:21

And they overcame him because of the blood of the Lamb and because of the word of their testimony, and **they did not love their life even when faced with death.**

~ Revelation 12:11 (emphasis added)

The point of bringing these things up is not to bring you down. Scripture declares that the law of sin and death has been destroyed. God doesn't want us obsessed by our thoughts of sin, nor with the thought of dying. That is freedom! If we are in fear, our vision has become obscured and we need to contend for His presence—a deeper *now* revelation of Jesus. The more of Him we get, the less conscious of sin and death we become. I once heard Bill Johnson say on a CD he was announcing his strategy for the next year. He said, and I paraphrase, "My strategy for moving forward this year is more of Him!" It truly is that simple. We always want the details. Jesus wants us to see our need for more of Him, and He will establish the details.

Obviously, people can die prematurely. That is why it is so important to stay on our path following Jesus and keep our hearts turned to Him. If we are following Him closely, then He will protect us, and nothing can stop us from fulfilling our destinies. We all have an assignment from God, and He tells us that anything which tries to rise up against it will not be able to stand. When we walk in our assignment, we are on our path. When we are on our path, we have a profound authority against anything that makes itself the enemy of our assignment. Our assignment in Christ is a superior reality than the contradictions that say otherwise.

One of my favorite westerns is *The Outlaw Josey Wales*. There is one portion of that movie in particular that I love. The great Comanche chief, Ten Bears, has taken two of the men from Josey's party and has made plans to attack the ranch where they were staying. Josey, being the brave cavalry soldier he was, got armed to the hilt and decided he was going to take the fight to Ten Bears. Before he left the ranch, Josey and the others knew they probably would not see each other again. Josey rode into the camp of Ten Bears, who was surrounded by his braves. Ten Bears came out and confronted Josey and asked him what he was doing. Josey basically said, "I've come to give you life or death. If you want life, we will take the sign of the Comanche and use it as our brand on our cattle. When you're in our area, you can slaughter some of the cattle and feed your people, and we can live in peace." Ten Bears said, "And if I don't?" Josey said, "Then I've come here to die with you today!" Ten Bears replied, "Because your words of death are true, I know your words of life are true—it will be life."

What this part of the movie speaks to me is that, when we are not mindful of death, the words of life that come out of our mouths possess a profound sincerity. Ten Bears knew Josey was sincerely not afraid to die. He respected that in a man. A man like that you can trust.

GROW UP IN THIS THINKING

I am learning to grow up in this thinking. As a man, and as a father, I know that I have some growing to do in this area because, while I might not be so mindful of my own life, I am very mindful of the lives of the ones I love. If something happens to me, I'm with Jesus. If something happened to my wife and kids, I know I would deeply grieve. Anyone who has a heart would, but because we know that we know Jesus, we shouldn't be ruled by a spirit of grief that would try to bring destruction.

A very dear friend of ours, Kris Walker, recently died of cancer. She was the wife of Phillip Walker, who played bass on my worship CDs. They have been close friends of ours for many years. Their children play with our children. Kris was and is a strong believer who fought valiantly to the end. She never wanted to die and leave her three young boys or Phillip. Together, they fought the good fight of faith, all the way to the end. Her bravery touched our entire church family and many others. When the doctors continued to bring bad reports, she boldly told them that she would live and not die, that she would declare the works of the Lord.

Money can't buy that kind of courage, and I am sure she had God's full attention. I prophesied life into her body. I prophesied her future, that she would be a homeschool advocate, and that she would write a book. Others that we did not know, who did not know what I prophesied, also told her that she would live and write books. We, along with many others, were in faith, but she didn't make it. In the natural, it would appear to be total defeat. It would look like she was not in faith, and I was a false prophet. I was tempted to feel like one. I even

132

apologized to Phillip because things did not happen like I said and how I was expecting them to.

So what I would like to suggest to you is that another possibility remains: what if her story is not over? What if she still lives? Most people can hardly see this way because they do not have this foundation at work in their lives at any level. Our minds are so wrapped around a temporal vapor that we miss the ocean for staring at the boat we are standing in! The only place we suffer loss is in this vapor of time. Yet we expend all of our energy and live as if this vapor is the beginning and the end. Jesus is the Alpha and the Omega, the author and perfecter of our faith (Hebrews 12:2). He will have the final word to say about Kris Walker's life and what she will do. We have eternal life now! We have to learn to think from an eternal perspective, because the Kingdom of Heaven is eternal. Jesus said for us to keep our minds on heavenly things.

Hebrews 6:1–2 says that eternal judgment and the resurrection of the dead are two of the foundational stones that the church is built upon. Foundation gives us strength to withstand the storms of life. When these foundations are operational in our lives, our eternal perspectives are increased. The more we have the revelation that God has eternally judged the law of sin and death, the more that law loses its power over our perception. Then we can see clearly, knowing we have a resurrection because of Jesus Himself, the hope of glory who ascended to sit at the right hand of God the Father, and He is in His glorified existence presently. He is our advocate that makes all this so. If sin and death have not been dealt with, with an eternal judgment, and there was no resurrection, then what hope would we have? Because of Christ, we have hope and now believe!

I don't want to pretend that I have arrived, but I do not want to pretend that I can't see the destination either. I'm choosing to set my face like flint, forgetting those things that are behind so that I might attain the prize. I have it by faith. So I walk and speak in the authority of the destination, not according to the contradictions of the present. I was born for this. You were born for this—to undo the works of the devil in people who are oppressed, to heal the sick, and raise the dead!

Kris Kristofferson wrote the song "Me and Bobby McGee," made famous by Janice Joplin. One line in the song says, "Freedom's just another word for nothing left to lose." That's not the whole truth, but it's a vital part of the truth. However, when we can effectively lay down our life in our hearts, the effects of loss can no longer rule over us. We are free to experience, with greater measure, a life that cannot be lost or corrupted as we follow Jesus. God is good, and He knows just what we need when we need it. He is making us. We are more than conquerors (Romans 8:37)! We are His workmanship created for good works in Christ (Ephesians 2:10).

CHAPTER 11

The Revelation of Reformation

It is time to put on your catcher's mitt in your hearts. As it has been said, "Some things are better caught than taught!" Everything I have said up to this point leads to what I'm about to share. It is the best wine that was saved for these last days, and it is the wine that will be given to the least. They will taste and see and know that God is good.

I am going to talk about the law of sowing and reaping, and the lie of sowing and reaping that is perpetuated by the enemy. The law of sowing and reaping is really not the point of the revelation I'm going to share, but it will be used to illuminate the revelation. So here we go.

Do not be deceived, God is not mocked; for whatever a man sows, this he will also reap.

~ Galatians 6:7

The law of sowing and reaping is a spiritual law that says if you sow good things, then you will reap a good harvest. If you sow bad things, then you will reap a bad harvest. That is pretty simple, and most religions believe in this law. Like the natural law of gravity that says what goes up must come down, these laws are effective; however, Jesus defied the law of gravity when He walked on water. If we look at the law of sowing and reaping from our natural perspective, we know that everything we do will put this law into effect. Make no mistake about it; this law exists in the earth. However, we are no longer of this world; we are only in it. We now live from another place, against which there is no law. God's intent for us was that we would not live in the fear of any law.

Many people who have lived a hard life, where they have abused themselves or others, may be born again. However, because they lived as they did, when they heard or read about the law of sowing and reaping, they then walk under the fear of what they have sown before they were born again. Even if they know they were saved by grace, and they know they are no longer under the law of Moses, they are still enduring the fear of what they have sown in their lives.

> *You foolish Galatians, who has bewitched you, before whose eyes Jesus Christ was publicly portrayed as crucified? This only I want to find out from you:* **did you receive the Spirit by the works of the Law, or by hearing with faith?**
>
> ~ Galatians 3:1–2 (emphasis added)

So, Paul no longer lived according to the past perceptions of his heart. He understood that he was crucified with Christ. When we are born again, we are all crucified with Christ, and we must have the revelation of

136

what that means, and receive the benefit of it. Jesus fulfilled every law. He satisfied God's judgment against sin and its punishment, and allowed Himself to endure it on our behalf. Jesus, also never being disobedient, never sowed bad seed. Therefore, the only harvest He could have possibly received is a harvest that is perfect in every way, right? But He didn't receive that. No, He received another harvest, a harvest that He did not deserve.

Whose harvest did He receive? Think about it. If He never sowed death, yet He reaped death, then whose harvest did He receive? He received *our* harvest! Yours, mine, and all others who would have eyes to see and ears to hear—he took our sin upon Himself, and He took the harvest of it. That is how He fulfilled the law of Moses, and the law of sowing and reaping, concerning His people. It is in the area of sowing and reaping we have one of the biggest battles with because most of us easily accept the fact that He saved us from our sin. Most of us know the law of Moses was fulfilled, but we don't realize the law of sowing and reaping concerning believers was fulfilled also.

HIS BEAUTY FOR OUR ASHES

When people get sick with something, everything in the earth is telling them it must be something they were exposed to, or something sown for in their lives. What we have to realize is that we have all sown for death, yet we receive His life. Jesus said that, if you hate your brother, you murdered him. If you look after another with lust, you've committed adultery. By statements like that, we all know we have all broken the law of Moses, yet we know, because of Him, we were set free from that law.

If you break the law of Moses, you sow bad seed, right? That means the only way to operate the law of sowing and reaping is to live up to the law. Since we know we cannot live up to the law of Moses, we cannot possibly live up to the law of sowing and reaping in our own strength.

Therefore, now that we are born again, something has changed. The entire perception of our being has been relocated and grafted into another tree—the Tree of Life. He is the vine, and we are the branches. When we are baptized into Christ, the benefits of our lives are now based on what He sowed when He lived in the Earth, and what He continues to sow through us presently. That is why we are enabled to receive His beauty for our ashes. That's why people receive His healing—because His healing is their healing. That's why Jesus walked on water. That's why the Holy Spirit quickens our mortal bodies and cleanses us of our sins. That's why, when the poisonous snake bit Paul, he did not die—because he no longer lived.

Death cannot kill what no longer exists. We deserve death, yet we live. Sickness cannot stay on Christ; it has already tried and failed. When we live and move and have our being in Christ, our bad harvest has no place to live, because Christ doesn't deserve it, and we no longer exist. We died with Him, and we were resurrected with Him! The life we now live is Christ's. That is a place for shouting a glorious praise to God!

Our old crucified nature has sown for a lot of things, but our new nature has already sown for another! The life we now live is Christ's, because our new nature is now His divine nature. We are new creatures in Christ. When we have this revelation, something happens to us. The law of sowing and reaping of our past nature no longer has a place to call home in us, because we no longer exist. The enemy is a master of knowledge when it comes to the law of Moses, the law of sowing and reaping, as well as the New Testament. He quoted Scripture to the Lord Himself when he tempted Him. When we become born again, according to grace, we are no longer under the law, and that would be any law that would come against who we are in Christ.

If you are born again, and the life you now live is Christ's, Jesus does not deserve what your old life has sown. Therefore, if you live in Christ, you reap according to the harvest He Himself has already sown for. My harvest now is according to what Jesus sowed, not what I have sown. Now, if I effectively live in Him, it is impossible for me to sow bad seed. But if I should fall, I can still get back in right alignment with Him now. When I do that, I have every right, as a son of God, to take ownership of the harvest Jesus sowed for. In Him, I find my refuge. In Him, I find healing, not according to what I have sown but according to what He has already sown. He is the sower of whose harvest I reap!

THE HOPE OF GLORY

The accuser of the brethren brings up what our old nature has sown to bring a sense of doom to us. He tries to imprison our minds by bringing up the past seed we have sown, to rob us of our hope. Then he tells us, "You better sow good seed and work yourself out of this dilemma, but you can't, because if you do that, you are trying to fulfill that very law in your own strength." But our hope is in the hope of glory Himself. Jesus is the hope of glory, who has sown for our future. We now live in the hope of the future He Himself has sown for.

If you are experiencing sickness, it has no right to be in your body because you no longer live, and the life you now live does not deserve it, because the life you now live is Christ's. If you are experiencing financial difficulty, it has no right to exist because you are dead, and now Christ lives, and everything good is His. Nothing evil, grieving, or bad has any place in Christ. This is where the battle of our faith is won or lost. The enemy is always trying to pull us out of this reality. When he cannot pull us out of this place of reality, freely given to us, we cannot be defeated!

> *I will not speak much more with you, for the ruler of the world is coming, and he has nothing in Me...*

~ John 14:30

Jesus was telling His disciples about His impending death. The enemy did come. Every evil, wicked, and sinful thing that the enemy could put on Him, including our sin and our harvest, was put on Him. The enemy did come looking to see what he could find, just as Jesus said he would, but Jesus told His disciples, *"He has nothing in Me."* So, when Satan and his evil horde came to see what they might discover, they could not find anything in Jesus because there was nothing in Him that was in common with them. What happened? He was resurrected! He took captivity captive!

So, when sickness tries to come upon you and the enemy tries to bring accusations against you, trying to imprison your faith, what is your defense? You can honestly say, "All this that you accuse me of may be true to my old nature, but that nature was crucified with Jesus, and I died with Him. Now I live in Him, and you were not able to find anything in Him then, and you cannot find anything in Him now. You no longer have a home!"

This is the revelation of His resurrection power, the revelation of reformation. Jesus is a redeemer. He came to redeem us from everything that comes from the evil wisdom of this age. Poverty has no place in Him. Sickness has no place in Him. Addictions have no power in Him. Generational curses have no place in Him, and you no longer exist, so what's a generational curse to do? They end, of course. They are superimposed by another bloodline. Now we reap where we did not sow! This is one of the most holy things there is to imagine. Think about it— we reap where we did not sow. Everything we receive from Jesus is according to what He did on the cross for us and where He is now, at the right hand of the Father in Glory. We receive from Him when we behold Him in His glory. He blesses us according to His riches in glory. When we behold the glorified Jesus that is on the other side of the cross, we reap His harvest! We are effectively living from Heaven to earth. Let it be on earth as it is in Heaven!

So, if we look at the law of sowing and reaping from our natural perspective, it produces, in its own way, the same works mentality that the law of Moses did—does it not? We are free from the law. The law of sowing and reaping does exist for those who have sown. The simple fact is, if you live in Christ, you no longer exist! The harvest of my old nature is now homeless. My new nature has a marvelous future! This is good news, isn't it? What could bring more *hope* than this? What could be more *dangerous* to the enemy than this? What could give you more *boldness* than this? What could give you more *freedom* than this?

The Scripture says, *"Do not be deceived, God is not mocked; for whatever a man sows, this he also will reap"* (Galatians 6:7). What does it mean, *"Do not be deceived, God is not mocked"*? What is the mockery that men and Satan participate in? Is it that they think they can get away with anything? Absolutely! It is true that you reap what you sow; however, if you are sowing from a fallen perception, what you perceive as good, what are you really sowing? You can't get away with living from this law any more than you can trying to keep the Ten Commandments. You also cannot get away from the effects of these laws if you are not exercising your faith in Christ. Whether you sow what men define as good seed or bad, if it comes from the nature of your fallen perception, you are sowing deception.

A lot of people try to use the law of sowing and reaping for their own gain. Yet the whole time they do, they may be living from their perception of the Tree of the Knowledge of Good and Evil and not the Tree of Life. If you live according to the law of sowing and reaping, as the beginning and the end of all things in your own power, you are essentially mocking what Jesus did on the cross, because the life you are supposed to be living now is His, not yours.

The law of sowing and reaping existed before Jesus ever walked the earth. If the law of sowing and reaping was your answer, you would have never needed Christ in the first place. If you couldn't live up to the law of Moses, why do you think you can live up to perfecting the law of sowing and reaping on your own? Many ministers and church people sometimes use the law of sowing and reaping, just like they use the law of Moses, and it casts doubt and fear over a person's life by warning them that they are going to reap what they have sown. If a person is putting their faith in that law according to their own strength, they need to be warned!

But if you no longer exist, and all things are now lawful, and the law of sin and death has been destroyed, and the life you now live is Christ's, and there are no laws against Him, and we now receive a harvest according to the seed He has sown…then where is the relevance of being concerned about the law of sowing and reaping? If your faith is in the law of sowing and reaping, and not the One who perfectly created and fulfilled the law, is that not mockery? How can you effectively live and move and have your being in Him, and not sow good seed? Jesus then and now only sows good seed. Even when He chooses to curse, it is good seed that is sown. That is why we must reckon ourselves dead to the contradictions that exist and that try to come against this present reality in Christ. When we can effectively live in the reality of living in Christ, the enemy is defeated. When we abide there, all the enemy can do is try to bait us up to fall out of this reality. It is impossible to effectively live in Him and not change into the glorious new creature that we are in Christ.

This is why healings and miracles do not occur like they should in our services. We teach that salvation is the free gift. We teach that by His stripes we were healed, now just believe. We teach that God's forgiveness to us is free to us when we receive salvation. We say that God's grace is undeserved favor extended to us freely. So, we teach that you have healing, miracles, salvation, redemption, and God's love by His grace. Yet when we teach about prosperity, we say you must put the law of sowing and reaping into effect, as if that is the only way you will be blessed! We teach that we receive everything else freely by grace through faith, except for our finances. On that subject, we teach that you must sow in faith for that.

YOU CANNOT SERVE TWO MASTERS

Do not get me wrong, anything that is not of faith is sin. But in effect, we are preaching grace through faith for some things, and law for others. We have become so blind to this that the notion of what I am saying is going to cause anger in the hearts of some, because the law of sowing and reaping has become a religious cow that some people serve. The Lord says you cannot serve two masters. You will end up loving the one and hating the other. People who preach the law, any law, normally despise the message of grace. You cannot effectively serve by teaching grace for some things and law for other things.

If you say I am preaching against sowing and reaping, you are wrong. I am not preaching against that law; I am preaching against our fallen perceptions of it. I am preaching that you can live in the Spirit of God in such a way that you do not have to be conscious of any law to follow the Spirit. For example, the punishment of sin is death. The law of sin and death has been satisfied because Jesus died that death for me. When I became born again, I died with Him, and I was raised with Him. If I no longer live, there is no law of sin and death for me. The law of Moses was fulfilled by Jesus because He never sinned. If He never sinned, and I no longer exist, then the life I now live fulfilled the law of Moses. If Jesus never sinned, then He never sowed bad seed. If I no longer live, my harvest from when I was carnal died with me when I died with Jesus. The life I now live is Christ's, so I reap now where I have not sown. That is the law of blessing in Christ! I have favor I do not deserve, that I did not sow for.

"Which is easier, to say, 'Your sins have been forgiven you,' or to say, 'Get up and walk'? But, so that you may know that the Son of Man has authority on earth to forgive sins"—He said to the paralytic—"I say to you, get up, and pick up your stretcher, and go home."

~ Luke 5:23–24 (emphasis added)

This is extraordinary grace. To Jesus, healing is the same as forgiveness of sins, and He said the Son of Man has the power to forgive sins! I have heard it said to some who were gravely ill that the reason they have not received their healing was because there was some sin they have not dealt with. That is such an ungodly statement. Where people come up with that kind of theology, I do not know. That does not line up with the Scripture above, or this one:

*Is anyone among you sick? Then he must call for the elders of the church and they are to pray over him, anointing him with oil in the name of the Lord; and **the prayer offered in faith will restore the one who is sick**, and the Lord will raise him up, and **if he has committed sins, they will be forgiven him**.*

~ James 5:14–15 (emphasis added)

Now, if you want to see how to sow for health, that can be found in the very next verse:

Therefore, confess your sins to one another, and pray for one another so that you may be healed. The effective prayer of a righteous man can accomplish much.

~ James 5:16

According to this Scripture, confessing our trespasses to each other, along with praying an effective prayer, releases healing among us. This is

145

His gift to us. If we are living in Christ, what else would we want to do? Confessing your sins is seen as an honorable thing. However, in most church cultures, you will be prosecuted for it. Not much healing can be expected in that environment.

WHEN WE BEHOLD, WE BECOME

The gifts of God, which are His salvation and Spirit that is given to us, are either free, or they are not. If you understand the revelation that all things are free to His sons and daughters, then you will know your perceptions of everything in the Kingdom will require His presence to fulfill your destiny. If you walk in the grace extended to you, and now you only do what you see Him do and say what you hear Him say, how can you sow bad seed? How do you not reflect the heart of God revealed in any law? Do you live in Him this way by focusing on perfecting the law of sowing and reaping, or by focusing on hearing every word that proceeds from the mouth of God presently? We must behold Him in His glory, presently. When we behold, we become.

To know God this way is what He has always wanted from man. Even when He told Moses to tell His people to get ready, His heart was to reveal Himself to them, at a level similarly to his revelation to Moses. He wanted His people to know Him as He is. But when He came down the mountain, and the people saw and heard the thundering and lightning, fear filled their hearts. They did not want to know God in such a way. So they told Moses, and I paraphrase, "We will die if we talk to Him; you talk to Him and tell us what we need to do, and we will hear."

The people were more concerned and interested in God's requirements for right-standing and blessing than they were about knowing Him for themselves. They did not want to be cursed. They simply wanted the blessings of God without knowing Him personally. When we seek after the principles and ways of God, above seeking after the personal relationship of knowing God, are we not doing the same things? Do we not simply want to know what we have to know in order to be blessed? Are we more concerned about being blessed than we are about knowing Him and accomplishing His will for our lives?

Later, while Moses was talking to God and the Lord was inscribing the stone tablets with His commandments, the children of Israel were making a golden calf for themselves. They said this was their god who delivered them from Egypt. When Moses returned to give them the Ten Commandments, he saw what the people were doing, and smashed the tablets. So, what do we glean from this story? They did not want to know God as He is, personally. They built for themselves a god that they were comfortable with, a god that they could serve as they wished, and they called their false god the one who delivered them from Egypt. We cannot, and we *must not*, create false images of who God is.

Let me ask you this: if you are a parent, do your children have to sow anything to receive your favor, blessing, love, honor, gifts, health care, or finances? Does their Christmas depend on what they have sown through the year? Do you quit feeding them if they act in a way you disapprove? Does the fact that you love and honor them instill in their hearts to do the same as you? Does how much you love and care for them inspire them to be obedient to you? Does your son have the authority and blessing of sonship in your house simply because he is your son? Or does he have to serve you in a particular way? Do you want him to serve you because he has to, or because he loves you and wants to?

> *"If you then, being evil, know how to give good gifts to your children, how much more will your Father who is in heaven give what is good to those who ask Him! In everything, therefore, treat people the same way you want them to treat you, for this is the Law and the Prophets."*
>
> ~ Matthew 7:11–12

According to Jesus's words in this Scripture, if we know how to give good gifts to our children, how much more will God give good things to us when we ask? That would be anything good that we want! It also outlines sowing and reaping in this Scripture, by saying whatever you want men to do to you, do also to them.

> *"In that day you will not question Me about anything. Truly, truly, I say to you, if you ask the Father for anything in My name, He will give you. Until now you have asked for nothing in My name; ask, and you will receive, so that your joy may be full."*
>
> ~ John 16:23–24

So, according to these Scriptures, do we receive from God by sowing, or by asking? When we ask, we receive. Does this fact take away from the reality of the law of sowing and reaping? No, it takes away from the consciousness we walk in, with regards to sowing and reaping. We do not serve the law of sowing and reaping; we serve God through Jesus, and the result is that good seed is sown. If we seek the Kingdom of God first, and His righteousness, will all these things not be added to us?

> *...And whatever we ask we receive from Him, because we keep His commandments and do the things that are pleasing in His sight. This is*

His commandment, that we believe in the name of His Son Jesus Christ,
and love one another, just as He commanded us.

~ 1 John 3:22-23

We receive, because we ask and keep His commandments. So, what are His commandments? Are they the Ten Commandments? Is it by perfecting the law of sowing and reaping? No, it is by doing what we see Him do, and saying what we hear Him say. It is living by every word that proceeds from the mouth of God. It is by encountering and living in Christ where we no longer live, and the life we now live is Christ's. Our Commander is alive, and we live out of this place where we actually hear Him now! We have a now vision of Christ; therefore, we do not perish. Now faith is substance! This is why He told me during the encounter that we must contend for His presence. When we live in the living presence of God, we receive what we ask for, because we are in the only place obedience can occur.

If you are not living in this place, then what you are being obedient to is a perception that was distorted by the wisdom of this age. We cannot know how to love properly without being in His love presently. When we have a revelation of His love presently, we are led to a place of repentance through His goodness. If it is His goodness that leads men into repentance, then when we see His goodness, we think according to what we are experiencing. It is in this moment that our perceptions are not distorted. To repent is to change from one way of thinking into His superior way of thinking. That is repentance. It is then that the axe has been laid to the root of carnal perceptions. That is why we must have our minds renewed by the washing of the water of His word. It is at this time

THE PRESENCE-PURPOSED LIFE

we are in agreement with Him and our own identity in Christ. We must become presence-purposed.

Remember the sheep and the goats on the Day of Judgment (Matthew 25:31–46)? The Lord told the sheep all the good things they had done, and they said, "Lord, when did we do these things?" They were not even conscious that they had done all these great things for Jesus. It was just who they were, so what else would they do? In the same way, we must do what we do because it is who we are. If we exercise conscious behavior toward doing good works above having a present relationship with Jesus, then our works become dead works. We are living toward what we want to be, instead of living from the finished work of who we are.

When we were born again, our carnal nature died. However, the demonic forces of hell and the remnants of distorted perception remain, so the perception of our minds must be renewed. The only way that happens is through our living, moving relationship with God. It is the present revelation of God that establishes right perception. We must exercise our faith to live in this place. This place is the prize of our lives. All the news is good in this environment, and we become like the environment we live in and behold.

Then our presence to others will be this same environment that changes and increases the perception of our hearts. When we know we are presently the holy dwelling place of God, anything we ask in His name will be done for us, so that our joy will be made full. From this place of relationship, all things are possible to those who believe! It is in this place that He has called us to live from. He wants us to fulfill the desires of our hearts. He even wants it to be more than we can think or imagine, so think big!

If you live lawlessly with a spirit of pride, then you will answer to the law as a law breaker. If you are someone who believes that they should keep the law, then you should see that you cannot. If you put all of your faith in the law of sowing and reaping, and not His grace, you will still be the target of all you have sown. If you are someone who is trying desperately and humbly to live in Christ, God doesn't see your failures; He sees your choice to live in Him in spite of the contradictions that exist in your life. He gives grace to you, which is undeserved, and it is according to what Jesus has already sown. You could sow what the whole world and all who are religious would perceive and agree is good seed and still be opposed by God. Why? Because God gives grace to the humble and opposes the proud. If you don't come to Him in humility to be born again with the purpose of losing your life to find His, then you will not be an effective partaker of His grace or His divine nature.

This only I want to learn from you: did you receive the Spirit by the works of the Law, or by hearing with faith?

~ Galatians 3:2

Selah.

Now, if you murder someone, and honestly become born again afterwards, there is the law of the land, and the harvest of what you have sown will bring men to prosecute you. But if you can learn to live in Christ, you will be like Paul, who was a free man even though he was in chains. When we put ourselves into those positions, God's grace will have to be enough for us—even if you are condemned to die in the electric chair. When you die, you would already be dead in your heart. That doesn't sound like good news to most of us, but if you are condemned to die, that is good news. It is men who prosecute, and they have to. Otherwise, how would you know who has honestly been converted or not?

When I was a deputy, we saw a lot of what we called jailhouse religion. Therefore, because in the world we are dealing with natural men, we must have the law of the land. We also may already be under the ravages of a bad harvest, but Jesus can set you completely free, and when you learn that you no longer exist, you will see the effects of your bad harvest evaporate. You can reckon yourself dead to your bad harvest now!

Once you are born again, you are now living in the present and the future hope of His glory. If you are not born again, or if you are but are not effectively living in Christ, then you live in *your* present and *your* past. For the unbeliever, it is literal; for the believer who lives after the flesh, it is in your mind, and it must be renewed. Romans 12:2 states, *And do not be conformed to this world, but be transformed by the renewing of your mind...*

This Earth and all who are of it are passing away. Everyone who is born again is ever-increasing in faith and newness of life, despite any contradictions that say differently. When we live in this place, the Kingdom of Heaven is released upon the earth. When someone hears you speaking from this place, the Kingdom of Heaven is being released upon them. If you have eyes to see and ears to hear, the Kingdom of Heaven is coming upon you now as you hear this word, because I do not speak of my own, but of Him who sent me.

When you are effectively living in Christ, you will still suffer persecution which could make you think you have sown for something awful. However, that is not always the case. Jesus said, "Remember, when they hate you, they hated Me first" (John 15:18, paraphrased).

> *"But beware of men, for they will hand you over to the courts and scourge you in their synagogues; and you will be brought before governors and kings for My sake, as a testimony to them and to the Gentiles. But when they hand you over, do not worry about how or what you are to say; for it will be given to you in that hour what you are to say. For it is not you who speak, but it is the Spirit of your Father who speaks in you.*
>
> *"Brother will betray brother to death, and a father his child; and children will rise up against parents and cause them to be put to death."*

> ~ Matthew 10:17–21

When we live in Christ, and truly have reckoned ourselves dead to our old nature, we will be the object of hate and persecution because the spirit of this age in religion, the world, and carnal men will not love or respect God or those who live in Him. Unfortunately, when Christians think carnally, they will sometimes attack also. That assault is not your harvest—it is because sin and death still reigns in the hearts of some men, even Christians. I want to challenge you with this: the word of God says that no man could take Jesus's life; He had to choose to lay down His life!

> *"For this reason the Father loves Me, because I lay down My life so that I may take it again. No one has taken it away from Me, but I lay it down of My own initiative. I have authority to lay it down, and I have authority to take it up again. This commandment I received from My Father."*

> ~ John 10:17–18

Okay, think about it now. It's no longer I that live, but Christ that lives in me. The life I am now living is Christ's, and He said no one takes His life but that He must lay it down of Himself. Wow, could it be that we are not living to the fullest of our Christian potential? Could I actually be so immersed in Him that I would have to choose to lay down my life in order for it to be taken from me? I mean, this could reverse Alzheimer's disease. This could stop the effects of cancer. We could actually be healed and renewed. This could reverse the aging process if it is true, right? I know you are saying, "This guy has lost his mind," but could it be that we have never tapped into the possibilities because we have accepted the deluge of fallen perception? I'm just trying to provoke your thoughts.

And Jesus said to him, "'If You can?' All things are possible to him who believes."

~ Mark 9:23

So, has what we have dared to believe, to this point, been corrupted by another perception? Is it that we can't believe beyond our carnal perceptions? We must break the barriers of this life with Kingdom perception. I want to challenge your faith. Because, after all, you are the one who says he believes Jesus was born of a virgin, that He was crucified on a cross, and rose from the dead, right? So, don't call me crazy if you believe that—either we are all crazy, or we are all sane! I love being insane for Jesus—I am crazy about Him!

REDISCOVER OUR FAITH

In order for us to be established in this new dispensation, we had better rediscover our faith. If you say that you believe in healings and miracles, how can you not believe that the aging process will improve, and Alzheimer's will not be reversed? Even our earthly medical profession is making strides in our longevity. They have more faith in their science than many of us have in our God. They refuse to quit, and we refuse to believe who we are called to be. We accept what they will not accept. These are just some of the barriers that have to be broken. God is calling this generation to break through the barriers that hold back His Kingdom. Lead, follow, or get out of the way! I'm going after God. If I bother you now, wait until next week. Wait until next year! I'm going to get worse to some and better to others!

If I'm insane, please leave me in my insanity, because I find eternal bliss here. I admit I'm crazy about the possibilities of living in Christ. It just amazes me that some of you can believe in a virgin birth, Christ's death and resurrection, and still believe that people who speak in tongues and believe in healing are crazier than you. Because to the natural mind, fallen perception, and the whole world for that matter, everything about Christianity is crazy, and, if you were sane, you would know that! But we no longer have a fallen perception; we have the mind of Christ, and we have to learn to live from this eternal position and not the wisdom of this age. We're either all insane or we are not. Once you cross the line of faith in One who was born of a virgin, you are as crazy as the rest of us. Perhaps I'm not as crazy as I look and sound, but that is debatable.

So, here is a scenario to stretch your thinking. Remember when I talked about someone who murders someone, but becomes born again after the event takes place, yet he finds himself ultimately on death row, and is sentenced to die on a particular day? What if they gave him his lethal injection but he didn't die? What if they rescheduled a week later, and the same thing happened? So they decided to put him in the electric chair, yet he lived through that also, without even a blemish? What if, then, one night he was worshipping the Lord, and the prison began to shake and his cell doors opened? And when he goes out of the doors, he discovers all the guards in the entire prison cannot see him, and so he decides to go to the grave of the man he killed, and raises him from the dead? I can already hear you saying, "Man, that's stupid. That's impossible!"

What if I told you that this has already happened, if you have eyes to see? Were not Shadrach, Meshach, and Abednego put into a fiery furnace, yet they lived? Did not Paul get bitten by a poisonous viper, yet he lived? Did not Paul and Silas worship the Lord in prison when the earth shook and opened the doors? Was not Peter in prison when an angel came and led him right past the guards, and he left? Did not Jesus raise Lazarus from the dead? After Jesus was resurrected, were there not others seen in the city who were known to be dead?

You may say, "Yeah, but the guy you're talking about was a murderer." One reason this story bothers us is that we want murderers to pay. God wants them transformed into His marvelous light where they no longer live in sin. As you should be able to tell, we have a perception problem. Many saw that Paul was responsible for the death of many Christians before he was converted. I can hear you saying, "Yeah, even still, your story was several different men, in several instances, over a broad period of time." But I say it was One whom several lived through by their faith! That One did these exploits through this group of men, the same One we are supposed to be living and moving and having our beings in. So, why would my hypothetical scenario be impossible?

BREAKING THROUGH BARRIERS

It is these barriers of our reasoning that we must break through, just like Chuck Yeager broke through the sound barrier. The Wright brothers broke through defying gravity with new laws—the aeronautical laws. One of the biggest barriers we have as Christians is to break through what other people on the outside of our situations think and say. The fear of man and our reputations with those must be crucified. We must break through our own man-pleasing barriers. For some it may mean that you have to break through your church-pleasing barriers. For some it may mean you have to break through your apostle-pleasing barriers. No, I am not speaking blasphemy. I'm speaking the truth. An obstacle to faith can wear any title, coming in the forms of family members, preachers, sickness, persecutions, lies, our own reasoning, and the like. When you know that you know that you are living in Christ, the obstacles will become clearer and clearer.

There are a lot of ministers who know that what I'm saying is where the Lord wants to take us. They are speaking these things. There are others who may not be able to write or preach these things because they may lose their ministry, but since I do not have anything to lose, I will speak on their behalf! Though I do not have anything to lose, I have everything to gain in Christ. It is our reasoning that stops the impossible because the impossible is always going to be beyond our reasoning, or it wouldn't be impossible.

Have you ever noticed that everything Jesus has ever asked us to believe is beyond what we call normal human reasoning? Jesus did not call us to be normal. He called us to do the impossible. One thing that separates Christianity from other beliefs is that we are supposed to demonstrate power over impossibilities. I do not want, in any way, to imply that I have arrived, but I have set my face like flint to press on toward the prize. I choose not to live in a place of hopelessness, despair, doubt, and unbelief. So I have decided to live in a place where my circumstances no longer rule or have relevance over my life. I have been doing this now for quite some time, and I recommend it for you as well. Hear my words!

We have to learn to live in the place where we behold Jesus in His glory. I can promise you this: anything He says for you to establish or reveal, or any exploit He asks of you—you can do it. Nothing can stop it but you. How do you know what God may suggest if you do not live in Him? How do you have power to overcome the things that rule in your life if you cannot live in Him?

That is why the revelation of grace is so important. When we come just as we are, He empowers us by His amazing love. If we don't spend time with Him, it is because we do not love Him properly. If we do not love Him properly, it is because we do not have a living revelation of His love. You may love Him as much as you can, considering where you live. But we must love Him with the love that transcends the contradictions of this world and ourselves. It is the love with which He first loved us. If we are in love with Him, then we will spend time with Him.

If you've lost that loving feeling, boldly go into the throne room of grace and humbly admit that this is where you are. Ask for help. He first loved you, or you would have never loved Him to begin with. He doesn't mind renewing your love. We have to go to Him for this, as an act of our will, because, as I have heard it said, "It is our passion that fuels our pursuit." When we behold Him in His glory, it is impossible not to have passionate love for Him. If you are His and you behold Jesus in His glory, you will follow Him with a deep passion for life. Remember: it is our passion that fuels our pursuit.

It is not enough to have a glimpse of this reality in Him. Many have had moments when they stepped into this place of glory. We must now get there and exercise our faith to remain there. We have to live in Christ effectively in order to live, move, and think like Him. It must be where we endeavor to live. He told me to contend for His presence, because, in His presence, I will experience the mind of Christ. In His presence, I will think like Him. In His presence, I will properly love. In His presence, I will be like Him. We must move into this greater realm of His glory. We must behold Him in His glory. We cannot faint now; we must move forward into this greater dispensation. It can be done. If you could only believe, all things are possible!

MY DECLARATION OF FAITH

I speak this by the Spirit of the Lord: I have come to be the enemy of everything that opposes this truth. I have come to set the captives free. Not as Jesus Himself, but as Jesus Himself did. I do not speak this in pride, but confidence. I am not ashamed for what He has done for me. I am not the enemy of men, but I may be the enemy of everything some men walk in. My conscience is clear to speak this way because I do not speak my words, but the words of Him who sent me.

He has sent me to set the captives free, to give sight to the blind, to preach the Gospel to the poor, to heal the brokenhearted, to restore those who have been crushed, and to proclaim the acceptable year of the Lord. This is the acceptable year of the Lord, and many of you have been starving for the words I am saying. My words will give life to you and keep you, because I do not speak my words but the words of Him who sent me. If you receive my words, you receive Him who sent me. For I did not come by my own accord, but by Him who sent me.

I was born for this acceptable year of the Lord, just as many of you were. This is the time to rise up and let the love in you rise again. Let your love rise to fill the way of life you're walking in, to find the joy inside when you were born again. I call the love in you to rise again.

A WORD FROM OUR LORD

You must no longer look at anyone after the flesh when they are living in Me. You must relate to them spirit to spirit. You must call upon that which you cannot see, as though it is upon them, to draw them to their future. You must lay the axe to the root of their fallen perception. That is who you are in Me—a warrior. You must no longer judge yourselves by your intentions and others by their works. You must not judge yourselves by grace and others by the law. You must no longer see yourself after the spirit and others after the flesh. You are either all of the Spirit, or all of the flesh! Do you not know that you are one body, the dwelling place of My presence? Why do you act as if you are not?

Live from the eternal place and contend for my presence. What can wash away your sins? Nothing but My blood. No longer call unclean what I have made clean. Very soon you will begin to see and hear what others before you were unable to bear. This is My good pleasure to do this, because

I have been waiting for this day since the fall of man, the day where you live in the place there are no laws against you, the day of My love, the day whereby all men can be qualified, and those who say they know but do not will be disqualified. This is the holiest of moments. When this is established in the hearts of My people and the world, My church as you know it will be forever changed in the earth. Everything you knew before will be quickened and upgraded to this higher level. My discernment in you will be at the highest level in the earth that has ever been.

If you think My grace is easy as some of you say, ask Ananias and Sapphira; they thought they could lie to the Holy Spirit and receive My favor by their contribution. In the place you are going, mockery will not be tolerated. The fear of Me is the beginning of wisdom. Do not lie to and mock what I have freely given to you. Do not blaspheme this holy place or each other, since you are holy as well. That is all I am asking of you. I died on the cross gladly to give you these things. It is My pleasure and My Father's pleasure to do this for you. I have longed for this day with My Bride. This acceptable year of dispensation will be the last before I return. Do not count this year as your earthly years. This is a year of the spirit of eternity, not time, which is passing away.

My prayer has always been that you would be as one, just as My Father and I are one, that you would be one with each other just as you are one with Me. Put away now your carnal perceptions and step into the place I have called you to and made for you. With all of your heart, contend for My presence and exercise your faith to reckon yourselves dead to the things of this world. They are no longer relevant to you. If you do this, what you need will be added to you. The birds of the air neither sow or reap, nor gather into barns. Yet your Heavenly Father feeds them. Are you not better than them?

I have already sown for your future. Now rest in Me; taste and see that what I am saying to you is true. If it was not, I would tell you. If you could have sown for your future, I would not have come. You cannot sow your way into My Father's Kingdom. You can either enter by the door, which is through Me, or remain outside of the door.

There is no other way to My Father except through me. If you live and move and have your being in Me, when the Father sees you, He sees Me. When the world sees you, they see me. When the enemies of God see you, they see Me. Because you have become one with Me, therefore, you are one with My Father, and that is His good pleasure, because My Father loves you. My Father wants to put His robe of sonship upon you. My Father wants to put a ring, the insignia of His household, upon your finger. My Father gives you the authority of His household as a son or daughter. My Father is well pleased with you because, when He sees you, He sees Me.

All that My Father has given to Me, I am giving to You. Nothing can separate you from My Father's love. My grace to you will not be overcome by the enemy. My love for you will not be overcome. My words to you will not be overcome. My goodness to you will not be overcome. It is the enemy who would try to add question to that. Do not listen to him; his days are fleeing him. The days of this world are passing by him, spinning like a vortex.

Some of you have chosen to be a slave to righteousness. Some of you have learned to be a servant. Some of you have even been an employee of My Father's Kingdom. Some of you have walked according to your legal rights. Some of you have learned to be a friend; some of you have learned to be a lover. Now you must learn to be warriors. Now you must learn to be My brothers and My Father's sons. Now you must also learn to be My Bride. Now you must learn to be My family with others of My Father. When you are family, there are no contracts; it is just who you are. You must now learn to walk in the privilege of My Father's house as a son or daughter. You must know the privilege of the secret place between the bride and the groom—the place where destiny is conceived.

Each age has had its own glory, but the world has never seen the fullness of the glory of this age. Before this time, only a select few have ever been able to reach some of these levels. Now it will be the commonplace of My Father's household. In this new season and the dispensation of this age, I will impart to you the revelation of these things at a greater level than you have previously experienced. It is necessary for the times you are now in.

This is not something that is coming; it is already here. You are well-equipped, My chosen ones. Look and see that I have made you mighty for the pulling down of the strongholds of the evil wisdom of this age. Do not be enamored by your power, though, or you will be hindered by it. I glory in you for this, and the world will see My glory upon you, and miraculous change will begin to occur because of My presence upon you. Contend for My presence, contend for My presence, contend for My presence!

This is a time where the different streams of My dispensations will converge into a river. This is the day of the multifaceted, manifold wisdom of God. This is the day of My pleasure in you. This is the day when meager possibilities will be overcome by radical impossibilities, a place where laws are defied by love, a place where My glory will be evident upon you. Receive My words and make them your words. This word will keep you and show you things to come. This word will increase you, and increase in you, if you have ears to hear and eyes to see. My faith is in you to do all that I ask you to do, and My faith does not fail because I never fail. Love never fails, and My love covers you. You are My chosen generation, whom I trust to do what I ask. I have waited for this day, and the day is now!

What you will begin to see now are the effects of My sword in the hands of a skillful wielder. You will begin to see and understand that I have overcome the world. And what I am overcoming through you is every kingdom that remains apart from me, from the inside out. The world and its wisdom always looks at the outside of everything, but I look on the inside. When the resident evil is destroyed, that which remains will be strengthened. This will be understood by individuals and kingdoms. To reform the Earth, We begin with you, then the church, and then the world. I did not come to bring peace on earth but a sword. You must become skilled with the weapons of My warfare. But you first must become familiar with Me.

When you live in Me, and have your being in Me, no longer can you only call the Kingdom of Heaven as merely My Kingdom. It must become your Kingdom as well. You must take ownership of your citizenship. You must take your privilege as a son or daughter in My Father's house. You can only give what you have to give. If you can't take ownership of who I've

THE PRESENCE-PURPOSED LIFE

called you to be, then you will be impotent to accomplish what I have called you to accomplish. You must know this. I will withhold nothing from you that you need to accomplish these things.

I have called you to a place of rest that, until now, very few have found. Everything from this point on will be accomplished by those who have found refuge in Me. What you will do is impossible to the world. What I have called you to do is scientifically impossible to men. But I would not ask you to do anything that was impossible for Me. Nothing is impossible through Me, and when you live in Me, nothing is impossible for you. If this were not true, I would not have told you these things to begin with.

Now is the appointed time for you. Now is the day of salvation and impartation, and I tell you the harvest is white and ready to be brought in. Who will go? Who will go into the fields and reap what I have sown for? Who will find the pearl of great price? Who will bring down the high places and raise up the lowly? Who will make the crooked paths straight? Who will say yes and let Me sanctify their yes? Who will take My beauty for their ashes?

Who said you could not do this thing that I ask? Where are your accusers, and who are they anyway? Where were they when I laid the foundations of the Earth? Where were they when I created man? Where were they, and who are they anyway? What is it to you, what they would say and think about you? Did they come to you and clothe you when you were naked? Did they feed you when you were hungry? Did they visit you when you were imprisoned? Did they stand with you when everyone else left you? Did they encourage you when all was lost? Did they bind up your broken heart? Did they put salve on your wounds? Did they affirm who you are in Me? Do you not only see these people when you are trying to break through your sorrows and present contradictions? Do they not come to question you, and try to sow their leaven into you? Do they not try to bring about doubt and confusion to you? Why would you be concerned about their opinions? Are they not being used by the accuser of the brethren to do his will, even if they say they have knowledge of Me? Do *you not know that you must keep going because you may be the only hope your naysayers have?*

Think on these things, and in all things be thankful. It is a miracle when people witness you in your hardships, yet you still insist on following and worshipping Me. These hardships are temporary, but I AM eternal, and you live in Me. Bear the fruits of one who lives in Me. Be discreet in the freedoms of your faith, causing no one to stumble except for those that I will to stumble. I AM the foundational cornerstone to some and the rock of offense to others. That is why you must know My voice and not rely on your own understanding. I have longed for this day, and you are My chosen generation—the royal priesthood of our Kingdom! Contend for My presence! Go now into the place that I call you to go and subdue the Earth for our Kingdom.

Wow, how do I follow that? With all of my heart, I suppose! Is God not incredible? Is He not the most surprising, loving, faithful, kind, generous, overwhelming Creator of all time? I am in awe. I don't know what you are experiencing, but it is good at my house right now!

CHAPTER 12

Coming Into the Knowledge
of Truth

I have spent thousands of hours reading Scripture, reading books, praying, worshipping, leading worship, listening to teaching CDs, and soaking in God's Word. I am telling you all of these things to say this: just because I have done all of these things does not mean that I have come into the knowledge of truth.

> *For among them are those who enter into households and captivate weak women weighed down with sins, led on by various impulses,* **always learning and never able to come to the knowledge of the truth.**
>
> ~ 2 Timothy 3:6–7 (emphasis added)

So, what does it mean to come into the knowledge of truth? When we hear this, we often think this means that we have finally figured it all out.

We now have a working knowledge of the word. We have learned the spiritual principles of God. We have studied to show ourselves approved, rightly dividing the word of truth, but is that what it means to have come into the knowledge of the truth? Two questions to ask *help* reveal the answer, or you could say the whole truth.

1. What is the truth?
2. Who is the truth?

The answers to these two questions *help* lead us to the answer that we are searching for. The word of God in the sense of Scripture is absolutely true. We can bank on what is said in Scripture; it is solid and holy. However, the Bible was not born of a virgin. It did not turn water into wine. It did not heal the sick and raise the dead. It did not suffer under the hands of Pontius Pilate. It was not nailed to the cross, nor did it declare that it is finished. It did not rise from the dead in three days. It is not seated presently at the right hand of God. It is simply the written word of God that we hold as canon. Scripture is the irrefutable word that we as Christians hold near and dear to our hearts. That is what we should do. So, how is it that Paul says that we are always learning and never coming into the knowledge of truth? What causes that?

The journey for the completion of this answer can be discovered in the second question. Who is the truth? In the first question—"What is the truth?"—the *what* came from the *Who* that is the truth. There was no Scripture written by men before the person of Truth spoke.

> *Jesus said to him,* "**I am the way, and the truth, and the life;** *no one comes to the Father but through me."*

~ John 14:6 (emphasis added)

Before there was any Scripture, there was God.

> *He is the image of the invisible God, the firstborn of all creation. For by Him all things were created, both in the heavens and on earth, visible and invisible, whether thrones or dominions or rulers or authorities—all things have been created through Him and for Him.* **He is before all things**, *and* **in Him all things hold together.** *And* **He is also the head of the body, the church;** *and He is the beginning, the firstborn from the dead,* **so that He Himself will come to have first place in everything.**

~ Colossians 1:15–18 (emphasis added)

With these two Scriptures, we can understand and know that the truth is Jesus. Jesus is the expressed image and the revealed will of God. He was with God in the beginning, and He was made flesh and dwelt among us (John 1:2, 14). Everything about the Father's heart toward us is found in His Son. So, we know Jesus is the truth, and the Scriptures are truth, inspired by the truth. How then do we come into the knowledge of truth? How is it that we can study the Scriptures, even serve and witness, yet never come into the knowledge of truth?

INTO HIS DIVINE NATURE

We can have an intellectual understanding of the things Jesus said and did (as revealed to us in Scripture) and still not possess the knowledge of truth. Until we become transformed from the remnants of our carnal mindsets into His divine nature, we have not come into the knowledge of the truth. What separates a man who knows the word of God and principles of God from one who has come into the knowledge of truth? One knows what Jesus said and has learned spiritual principles, while the other no longer lives. The second man lost His life to find life; he lives and moves and has his being (Acts 17:28) in the One who is truth personified.

> *You are our epistle written in our hearts, known and read by all men; clearly you are an epistle of Christ, ministered by us, written not with ink but by the spirit of the living God, not on tablets of stone but on tablets of flesh, that is, of the heart.*
>
> ~ 2 Corinthians 3:2–3, NKJV

We do not fully come into the knowledge of the truth until we become one with Christ to the point where we have His word written on our hearts, not just memorized with our heads. We must do this if we desire to fulfill our destinies and bring the Kingdom of God to those around us. Anything less is lip service—smoke and mirrors. It is having a form of godliness but denying its power (2 Timothy 3:5). To come into the knowledge of the truth, we must enter into the person of Christ, who is the word of truth. We do this by worshipping Him in spirit and truth— and I'm not just talking about a good worship service at church. When we behold Him in His glory, He is revealed to us. Jesus Himself said that if we abide in Him and His word abides in us that He would manifest Himself to us. Jesus will manifest Himself to us! When is the last time Jesus manifested Himself to you?

So what does it look like to become a living epistle of Christ? Do we have to be perfect? Do we have to know all of the Scriptures? Do we have to be whipped or tortured? Do we have to be celibate? Do we have to be rich? Do we have to be poor? What must we do to be a living epistle?

You can become a living epistle immediately—the moment you are born again. In fact, most new believers are closer to this point when they are first born again because they are in love with God and their relationship with Him is fresh. The problem and the solution, for most of us, is that God wants us to grow up into that love which we have been born into. We must become consistent in our pursuit and determination to live in Him. Staying in alignment with the Spirit of God must be our first priority. This is where we stumble because the remnants of our old nature still like to admire other gods. God wants us to learn to abide in the vine. We must give Him preeminence in our lives. I am not talking about reading the Word, though that is a part of it. I am talking about abiding in the spirit of the word made flesh—the Spirit of Jesus—so that His word becomes written on our hearts and our lives become living epistles. Many read the Scriptures and become scholars, but few are transformed by them to the point that they actually embody the Spirit of Jesus and become living epistles. Through Christ, God has enabled us to become participants in His divine nature (2 Peter 1:4). Are you participating in His divine nature, or merely studying it? The first makes you more like Christ, but the latter leaves you with a big head and a small heart.

THE PATH OF GREATNESS

The cross we bear is staying in love. The cross we bear is laying down anything that tries to come in between us and our life in Christ. The only way to successfully stay in Christ is to stay humble and receive the grace that comes from Him. He gives grace to the humble but resists the proud. So how does this happen, this pride? I am so glad you asked! We love flattery. We love being looked to as the answer. We love being seen as the answer to everyone's problems. We love being the object of attention. You know, all the things Lucifer loved. We become ensnared by our own desires of greatness.

Make no mistake about it, we were born for greatness. However, the path of greatness is not the path the world follows. The path for greatness in the Kingdom is laying down our lives to find life. The path of greatness in the Kingdom is esteeming our brother higher than ourselves—you know, all the things most of us do not like. This sounds unreasonable, and it is to our natural mind; hence, our minds must be renewed by the washing of the water of the word. This is not necessarily predominately Scripture, but also the proceeding word that comes from the mouth of God—presently. We must not let anything win the battle for our hearts and minds. This is where the warfare is, and this is where the great exchange of life occurs. Our carnal nature is slain, while His nature is increased. Then we are blessed and highly favored! Anything that tries to come between this great exchange is an idol, and idols must be smashed!

So, how do idols get into our lives? You ask some really good questions! Idols work their way into our lives by enticing desires that already exist in our lives. For example, imagine you are a Christian man. You have been married fifteen or twenty years. Your wife may be a bit of a nag, and since she has had three kids, you feel taken for granted. You go to work, and this new young lady starts to work with your company.

You noticed that she looks at you as someone important. Then you begin enjoying the company of this person who sees you as valuable. Before long, you are helping her with her work, and you begin to become friends. Of course, you're just friends, because, after all, you are married. Then you become smitten, because you are sure this woman loves being around you. Your ego is being inflated at light speed. You find yourself thinking all the time about this woman with whom you are smitten. In fact, you have even started working out again and being conscious of your appearance when you go to work. You begin to feel like, "I have still got it. I have arrived."

Meanwhile, back at the house, your wife is still unaware of your existence. It seems like she couldn't care less. What is important to you seems to get on her nerves, but this new girl seems to love everything about you. So, you are drawn even more to this young lady, because she makes you believe only you can rescue her. You no longer can tolerate the thought of someone else being the one who might rescue her. You think that to just hold her and tell her you are here for her would be so wonderful. You love how she makes you feel, how she smells. Your senses are filled with her presence, and you can no longer resist her. That is one example.

Here is another example: You are just becoming an adult. You are finally out on your own, and you are realizing the freedom and authority you possess. You are no longer under the scrutiny of nosy parents. You have come of age, and you decide to go out and enjoy this world as a man. As hard as you are trying, though, your bills are now piling up, and you find yourself struggling. You get overwhelmed with life and begin to feel down. You start seeing how hard it can be to live on your own. But you live in this new apartment complex, and it is filled with others like you. The younger crowd seems hip and full of purpose. You begin to meet these new friends. They are different from the ones you used to hang out with. They seem to be free spirits, without a care in the world. They also party and do things you were not permitted to do. They assure you it is safe to do these things, and that parents and responsible people are just sheltered. All those things your parents told you about alcohol and drugs were just myths propagated by them to control you and make you like them.

So, you decide to experiment with your curiosity, because let's face it, you are now a man, and you can do anything you like. You control your destiny, and no one else has authority over you. When you take this new drug, it is wonderful. You think, "Man, I could have been doing this for years." You love how it makes you feel—free of all the burdens. You do not know which is better: the freedom you have to take the drugs, or the way the drugs make you feel. You feel as if you have arrived into adulthood. You are proud of yourself for becoming your own man.

Here is another example: You are born again, and you love God. You have a beautiful voice, and you are a great musician. You can write songs, and the anointing of God is profound when you minister. Then, as you are developing in your walk with God, you realize that you are called to be a prophet. You get so excited about what you have been called to. You begin to get calls to minister, and when you go, they see your calling also, and they tell you how profound you are. You are so amazed and blessed by God that you just feel like you are walking on air. You continue to get calls; however, this time, they are referring to you as a prophet.

Now everyone's attention is focused on you. You are the one—the one who delivers the word of God himself. You begin to demand that those around you submit to who you are, assuring them that they will get the reward for doing this because you are the anointed one chosen by God. You begin to build everything around who you are, because who else could be discerning enough to lead the people other than you? You begin to reject those around you who do not obey you with lightning speed. You start to listen only to those who speak of your greatness. You become enamored with who you are in Christ, and less enamored with who Christ is in you. Because it is you, the chosen one, who speaks, you begin to flatter people in your group so that they become enamored of you as their leader. You know, if you do this, they will do anything you ask. They will serve you with everything they have. They will love who you love, and turn on those you turn on. They will submit themselves fully to your rule, and reject others who do not. In fact, no one else has anything worth hearing. Because anything else, besides what comes from within this holy alliance you made for yourself, is not as spiritual as you and what you are already hearing. Now you are the head of your church, where you believe you belong!

All three of these stories are about people who get enticed by their own desires. When you are enticed, you are led away by your own desires.

Blessed is a man who perseveres under trial; for once he has been approved, he will receive the crown of life which the Lord has promised to those who love Him. Let no one say when he is tempted, "I am tempted by God"; for God cannot be tempted by evil, and He Himself does not tempt anyone. But **each one is tempted when he is carried away and enticed by his own lust.** *Then,* **when lust has conceived, it** *gives birth to sin; and when sin is accomplished, it brings forth death.*

~ James 1:12–15 (emphasis added)

There are stages in the process of sin and the death that it brings. Temptation is not sin, or Jesus would be a sinner, because Scripture says that He was led into to the desert to be tempted by Satan. To be tempted is to be brought into a place of desire by that which want to have. Jesus was tempted; however, He never allowed His desires to conceive. When He was enticed by what He discerned was an idol, He smashed that idol by resisting it and His tempter, and He walked away from it. Afterwards, it says that angels came and ministered to Him (Matthew 4:1–11). So withstanding some of the temptations of life is no easy thing. But I will tell you this from experience—anything beyond resisting temptation will prove to be harder on you, not easier. If the Father sent angels to minister to His Son after He refused the enticement, and not passing the test is worse, then what do we do when we fall to temptation?

BLINDED BY THE BLISS

When we fail the test, we have a season of ecstasy when sin has its pleasure. In our pride we have been overtaken by our desires and have conceived sin. It is in this place where you are most blinded by the bliss of that you have become enslaved to. You cannot hear sound reason. No one can get through to you. Your perception is completely distorted, and you are imprisoned. You just so happen to be in love with a prison, though you do not realize it. It does not matter what you did to get there, or even what it was you were doing. The end result is that you have become the slave of that which you have chosen to obey. What can be done for one such as this?

In 2 Samuel 12, the prophet Nathan confronts David in his sin. David knew in his heart that he had sinned against God. He fell on his face and repented with deep grief. He had already made Bathsheba his wife, so he had to live with the consequences. However, because of his heart, God restored a right spirit within David. God is such a restorer that the later result of David and Bathsheba's union was the birth of their son Solomon, David's successor to the throne! Now, if some of our talk shows could have gotten their hands on David, he would have been publicly humiliated by the studio audience. He would have been slammed by the media and forced to abdicate his throne. He never again would have had any credibility. He certainly would not be invited to our church services to sing his psalms.

It is hard to help someone who is in the season of pleasure that their sin provides. It is hard to smash the idol that you are in love with. If there is anything you do not want to do, it is to destroy the thing which brings so much joy to you, the one who made you feel different and more alive than anything you have ever encountered. As I have already said, no one gets away with anything. A measure of death is released over and into everything we are connected with. In some cases, it is a literal cessation of life. Whether the person sees it or not, sooner or later, all they will see is the prison that remains. Since our sin was dealt with on the cross, it is not so much that we have fallen into sin, in the sense of separation from God, as much as we have fallen from the high position of living and moving and having our being in Him. So, essentially, we have fallen from grace. For Christians, the issue is not sin, because all things are lawful.

FULLY LIVING IN CHRIST

The issue for Christians, when it comes to fully living in Christ, is whether or not we are going to worship idols. Now, those can be what many would identify as sin, but they can also be what many would call good things. For example, take the story of Mary and Martha. Jesus was in the house. Mary sat at His feet and beheld the Lord. Martha was in the kitchen serving and washing dishes—as well as becoming agitated with Mary. It would seem that serving would have been the thing to do, but Jesus told her that Mary chose the best part, and He would not deny her what she desired (Luke 10:38–42). Martha chose well, but she did not choose the best part. When we live in Christ, He is always leading us to the best part. The enemy will use good parts to keep us out of the best part. The enemy will use what many would call a *good* thing to keep us from the *best* thing. So, how do we know what is the best? *Jesus* is the best part. When Jesus is with you, as He was with Martha and Mary, choose Him and you can't go wrong! We will come back to this later.

The next stage of the effects of sin that I want to discuss is the imprisonment. I have never heard an addict boasting of their addiction, unless they had been turned over to a reprobate mind. Most drug addicts, alcoholics, perverse sexual addicts, and the like normally are not proud of their addictions. The pleasurable season has long passed, and they have been diminished to ruins. They know they are a mess, and many are very contrite and lowly of heart—until they need their next fix. Then they will possibly kill, hurt, or deceive anyone who would come between them and what they desire. They turn into a predator of their desire, and they will lie, cheat, or steal to have it. They have been taken captive by the enemy to do *his* will, and now they kill, steal, and destroy. This is no longer done in pride, but a dark, driving necessity that screams and twists in their gut and the members of their flesh. They become dangerous to themselves and those around them.

Obviously, not all who are addicted may be as extreme as I just described, but at some level, whether they admit it or not, these things are happening. In this place, these types of people are where they can hear, believe it or not. Because pride and pleasure are usually out of the way, they know they are a mess; they see and recognize truth much easier than those whose vision is blinded by the grandeur of their delusions. With that out of the way, truth can easily lead someone out of prison. It may be instant, or it may take some time. However, since all can come into the throne room of grace, just like they are, they can receive help to overcome their addictions.

People in these types of groups must know these three things:

1. God loves them presently, just as they are.

2. They must become born again, or if they are born again, they must make a fresh commitment to God.

3. They must know, in spite of their addiction, they must learn to reckon themselves dead to their condition, so they will feel free to boldly go into the throne room of grace to encounter Jesus, because the only thing that changes anyone or anything is an encounter with Jesus.

Now, here is a mystery that works well also. As Bill Johnson says, it is the one-step program. If we walk in the anointing, whether someone is born again or not, people can be healed, delivered, born again, and filled with the Holy Ghost, just from encountering the anointing on our lives. I saw two drug addicts get delivered from drugs, become born again, be filled with the Spirit, and speak in tongues, when they knew nothing of the things of God. They just happened to be at a meeting where a minister was ministering truth under the power of the Holy Ghost. Now that is power from Heaven to earth!

Here is the bottom line of all this: for all who believe in God and love Him, He causes all things to work together for our good (Romans 8:28). If you are addicted, He will use your addiction to teach you and raise you up in your bonds to be set free in all ways. If He is using your addiction, you may as well use it for your good also. The enemy is using all these things for your destruction. When we are carnally-minded, we are tossed to and fro between the intentions of the two kingdoms: the Kingdom of light, which is God, and the kingdom of darkness. You must choose to exercise your faith in God to overcome your addiction, or agree with the enemy and be destroyed by it. Your addiction cannot keep you from getting to God for help, because, if it could, you would be hopeless. You cannot get power to overcome without getting to Jesus, and He has opened the door to all who ask of Him.

Therefore, God wants you to reckon yourself dead to your sin and circumstances, so that you can overcome your sin and circumstances. This is the good news. If anyone speaks to you another gospel than this, they are lying to you. It is impossible to encounter Christ, dwell in Him, and not be cleansed, changed, empowered, enlightened, and become full of joy, peace, and righteousness in the Holy Ghost! Will you now believe this word I have given you? I promise, if you do these things, you will not fail!

KEEPING YOUR ALIGNMENT

Before I get started on this subject, Graham Cooke has perhaps one of the best teachings on this subject that I have ever heard. I would recommend that you hear him minister on this. However, since he is not with me, I need to touch on this subject because it is critical for our success. When we understand that we are born again, we should be taught that we have the privilege of living and moving and having our being in Christ, just as we are. When we capture that revelation in our hearts, we have arrived to a place in Christ where the process of impartation and transformation can begin to occur. In other words, it is in this place where we learn to grow up into Christ, whom we love. It is the fact that we are in love with Him, because He first loved us, and that love is what we are to grow up in. It should not decrease; it should only increase. What brings increase to our love for God is abiding in Him. When we become focused on abiding or living in Him, our love and vision increase. The knowledge which we have come into increases. The blessing and favor of God in and on our lives increases. What is the enemy of what I have just described? It is our lack of determination to resist the enemy's efforts to thwart our holy communion with God. That is where our spiritual warfare must be directed.

The Scripture says that the cares of this life choke out the word of God. What are the cares of this life? What is it that seeks to bring us out of the alignment of effectively living, moving, and having our being in

Christ? There are many things, but I will list a few: financial stress, sickness, addictions, traumas, sin-consciousness, law-consciousness, idolatry, envying, coveting, wrath, hate, unforgiveness, self-seeking, pride, false teachings, gossip, unfaithfulness, selfishness, what the world says is right, what the church may say is right, what your grandma always said was right, what your daddy always said was right, and so many more. Who are the carriers of these things? Our wives, husbands, children, preachers, elders, deacons, bosses, neighbors, friends, doctors, lawyers, judges, criminals, lovers of themselves, unreasonable men, the evil wisdom of this age, demons, fallen angels, bad spirits, principalities, powers of darkness, wickedness in high places, and the like.

IN THE SWIRL OF CONFUSION

Now, flesh and blood are not our enemy, but the perception some people are walking in may be the enemy of our communion with God. So, we must learn to hear His voice. When we find ourselves in the swirl of confusion, we must ask ourselves, "What does this mean, and what must I do? God, what are you trying to reveal to me in this situation?" It may take a day or so, but God will not leave you unanswered. He will reveal what is trying to corrupt your communion with Him and your personal transformation process. We have our confidence in the fact that we are joyfully living in His approval. It is that standing in Him that we must fight for. To paraphrase Graham Cooke, "It is one thing to arrive in such a place; it is another to remain there." God wants us to be transformed into someone who can remain in Him, even when everything around us contradicts the reality of where we live. When we can do that, we will demonstrate the love and power of God in every circumstance of life. When others see us in our circumstances, they will see Jesus.

Just this week, I had to make a decision that the world may consider wrong, and many Christians would think was not of God. My oldest daughter was graduating from her second year of ministry school. The school was in another state. We were not able to afford to go, and our only vehicle needed some repairs. I could have made it happen; in fact, we made the reservations, and were planning to go. But something inside was feeling out of order. Something was amiss for two or three days. I found it hard to write. So, I began to seek God about it. When I started writing this book, the Lord told me one thing: I could not let anything distract me from writing what He would tell me to write until I was through. He reminded me of this, and I knew that I was being distracted from what He asked me to do in the beginning.

Now, understand something here. I love my daughter, and I would do anything for her. I also knew my wife was not going to be happy because she had it in her heart to go, but I knew I must share what I believed the Lord was telling me. I sat down and began to share with Christy what I believed the Lord was showing me. She was sad, but she knew that this was a hard decision for me also. I called my daughter, and she was sad too, but she said she understood and was fine. Though I was torn between my flesh and spirit, I felt a sense of peace again, and found my alignment with the Lord was restored. My ability to write also increased again. This is why it is so important to keep our communion with the Lord free of obstacles that try to cause us to stumble. Our future and destinies hang in the balance with our being in alignment in our relationship in Christ.

Mary and Martha make for a great story that captures the heart of what I believe God wants to say to us. When the Lord is in the house, and He is speaking, we must behold Him, not worrying about our service. There is always a time to serve, but when He shows up, it is time to listen. When our local churches learn this, you will see great wonders transpire. Even our compelling drive to feel what we must do in order to please God can become the enemy of God. It is a religious spirit that would lead us to believe our service is godlier than beholding Jesus when He is with us. We must be conscious that it is the beholding which enables us in the becoming. We become what we behold. In other words, when we behold Jesus in His glory, we become enabled to be as He is in this world. When we become as He is, then our service will be worth something. Here is a great Scripture that captures the heart of what I am saying.

> *Then the disciples of John came to Him, asking, "Why do we and the Pharisees fast, but Your disciples do not fast?" And Jesus said to them, "The attendants of the bridegroom cannot mourn as long as the bridegroom is with them, can they? But the days will come when the bridegroom is taken away from them, and then they will fast."*

> ~ Matthew 9:14–15

For us now, there are seasons where we must fast, but there are also seasons when He shows up in His manifested presence. When this happens, we need to be fully tuned in to everything that proceeds from His mouth during the encounter. These types of encounters are always directly linked to His purposes in us and in the earth. In these moments, we are enabled to receive the impartation for change and the empowerment that we need for the next season. This is not to say that our personal fellowship in Christ is ever lacking. I am now speaking of when He manifests Himself to us, whether it is as an individual or corporately. In that moment, it is time for our mouths to shut, and our eyes and ears to open. It is time to receive and behold Him in His glory. We do not have to fast when He is manifesting Himself to us. We fast when He is not manifesting Himself to us, unless He directs us otherwise. God will remove His manifested presence when leaders try to corrupt the atmosphere with their religious mindsets, or they try to capitalize on the occurrence for their own gain. That is a fatal error. When God is manifesting, He does not need our help. He may use someone who is mature to guide others in this event, but that person is one who would not touch what the Lord Himself is doing.

To stay in alignment with the Holy Spirit, we must stay in the place of humility and allow God to make the changes He requires in us. God is no longer going to tolerate pretenders. That is not to say He is requiring our perfection, but He is requiring our full attention to the process of transformation—whether it is our individual walk with Him or our corporate gatherings.

CHAPTER 13

The Art of Being

NAMES OF GOD

And God said to Moses, "I AM WHO I AM"; and He said ... "This is My name forever, and this is My memorial-name to all generations."

~ Exodus 3:14—15

Him who is and who was and who is to come...

~ Revelation 1:4

"I am the Alpha and the Omega...who is and who was and who is to come, the Almighty."

~ Revelation 1:8

"I am the first and the last, and the living One."

~ Revelation 1:17b–18

"I say to you, before Abraham was born, I am."

~ John 8:58

"I am the door."

~ John 10:9

"I am the good shepherd."

~ John 10:11

"I am the resurrection and the life."

~ John 11:25

"I am the way, and the truth, and the life."

~ John 14:6

"I am the true vine."

~ John 15:1

"...they are not of the world, even as I am not of the world."

~ John 17:14

"I am He."

~ John 18:6

With all these Scripture references, it is easy to see the many aspects of Jesus. I hope to bring to light the very essence of who He is. When Jesus was walking the earth, He was not hoping to be something wonderful. He was not trying to just make it through the day, hoping that all would be well. He was not trying to be someone—He was *being* someone. Now, if you caught what I just said, there is a big difference between *trying* to be something and actually *being* it. Eternal life is not a carrot on a string that we are following behind, in the hope that we reach a divine destination. Eternal life is *now*, presently. Jesus was eternal in everything He did. His entire purpose was eternal in nature. He could not help but be who He was. Paul says something profound:

> **Let this mind be in you, which was also in Christ Jesus**: *Who*, **being in the form of God, thought it not robbery to be equal with God**: *But made Himself of no reputation, and took upon him the form of a servant, and was made in the likeness of men…*

> ~ Philippians 2:5–7, KJV (emphasis added)

Jesus did not consider it robbery to be equal with God. Why? Because He was God. He was with God in the beginning, yet He was also a man. All things are held together by His word! Paul says in this Scripture for this mind to be in us. What mind was that? The mind of Christ! But that is not all—it goes on to say what His mind was. He did not consider it robbery to be equal with God. I can hear you saying, "Wait a minute, brother; you have gone too far!" Have I? If I no longer live, and the life I now live is Christ, is Christ not equal to God? I know that I am not the person of Jesus Christ, but the person of Jesus Christ is the life I live. Jesus said He of Himself could do nothing.

> *Therefore Jesus answered and was saying to them, "Truly, truly, I say to you,* **the Son can do nothing of Himself**, *unless it is something He sees the Father doing; for whatever the Father does, these things the Son also does in like manner."*

> ~ John 5:19 (emphasis added)

THE PRESENCE-PURPOSED LIFE

We of ourselves can do nothing, yet with God, all things are possible (Matthew 19:26). So, where do you think God wants us to live in our minds? Do you think He wants us to think that we can do nothing, or that all things are possible? God wants us to know all things are possible, and that all of the things that pertain to life and godliness are impossible without Him. We must *know* it; we must not just *think* it. This is not theory; it is the superior reality of His Kingdom. We must know who we are. We either *are* or we *are not*. We must be now, presently, the righteousness of God in Christ! We must be willing now. When we are in Christ, led by the spirit of God, we are the sons of God. We cannot see ourselves as less than who we are. We become who we behold. If we behold Jesus in His glory, by His revealing Himself to us, then we become the likeness of His image here on earth. When He reveals Himself to us, we are revealed with Him in glory! When we are effectively in Him, where we no longer live, we do not have to consider it robbery to be equal with God. He created us for this! If He gives us the right, it is not theft but a gift! If someone gives you a gift, you do not have to consider it robbery that you possess what was given to you. No, I do not think I'm God. I simply believe I am a son of God. Believe on His words, and they will give you life!

THE LAW OF BEING

> **For whoever has, to him more shall be given**, *and he will have abundance; but* **whoever does not have, even what he has shall be taken away from him**.

> ~ Matthew 13:12 (emphasis added)

I say this by the spirit of God. I am, and I am becoming, like Jesus. I am presently, and I am becoming, more like Him every day, in every way. Because He is the author and perfecter of my faith, I go from faith to faith and glory to glory. This is who I am. My present reality is in Him, and my future is in Him. All things are possible now because I am in Him. He is the Alpha and Omega, and I am living the life of the Alpha and Omega, presently. Because I have, I will have more. If I do not have, what I have will be taken away from me. I do not give so I will be blessed; I give because I am blessed. Because I am blessed, I will be increased with blessings. If I am not blessed, then what I have will be taken from me. This is the law of being in Christ. By His stripes I am healed. Because I am healed, I will increase in divine health and heal others. If I am not healed, then what health I have will be taken from me.

If I have what I am believing for now, it cannot be taken from me. Because I am in Him presently, I can legally live in my destination. My destination is to be in His presence, therefore, I live in His presence now! I am the righteousness of God in Christ. I am a new creature. I am a new species in Christ Jesus. I have the mind of Christ. I am in Him, and He is in me. I am His beloved and He is mine. I am patient and kind because He is patient and kind. Because I am patient and kind, my patience and kindness is growing. If I am not patient and kind, then what patience and kindness I have will be taken away from me. I am, and I am becoming, like my Lord. So, who are you?

> For nothing is hidden that will not become evident, nor anything secret that will not be known and come to light. So take care how you listen; for whoever has, to him more shall be given; and whoever does not have, even what he thinks he has shall be taken from him.

~ Luke 8:17–18

True revival occurs when a person or a group of people come into *being*, when they live in the *I AM* of who God is in them. On the day of Pentecost, we often picture the scene as the Holy Spirit descending upon the people, and they were empowered. That is true, but something even greater happened than the limited vision of that description. Not only were they empowered, but they also all came into a new place of *being*. Their existence changed. They were no longer the same people, in the sense of *being*. Peter rose up in this place of *being* and preached a message, and three thousand believers were added to them. Wow! That is power! He basically said *this* is the *that*, which the prophet Joel prophesied would happen. He was saying *this is* in the power of *I AM*.

We sometimes describe revival as when someone is set ablaze with the power of God. It is true that, when someone becomes a burning bush, they are experiencing revival, or renewal; however, historically, these fires seem to wane. God wants to raise up a generation that learns to live in this place for the rest of their lives. In the past, we have accepted this kind of reality as seasonal or occasional, eventually returning to the real world. I would like to suggest to you that this is a lie from religious spirits, the world, even hell itself. This world is not the real; it is the counterfeit. There is nothing more real than God Himself.

THE KNOWLEDGE OF BEING

Everything that you see with your natural eye was created from the invisible. But just because we do not see the invisible with our natural eyes does not mean that it does not exist. Not only that, in the Spirit we can see it. We do not see gravity, but we see the effects of it every day we live. When we see and hear in the Spirit, we manifest the Kingdom of God into the natural realm. Then we are establishing the Kingdom of Heaven on earth. We have to come into the knowledge of *being*. When you come into the knowledge of *being*, you come into the knowledge of Christ. It is not knowing *about* Christ; it is the knowledge that comes from *being* in Him, being in *I AM*. When you experience who you are in Christ, you are as He is, Christ revealed in His glory, Christ revealed in you.

This cannot be taught; it has to be caught! I can lead you to this reality, but I cannot *be* you for you. You must *be* in Him yourself. Now, if I am in Him, you have a great shot at *being* in Him yourself because I will be releasing the power of where *I AM*. In fact, the greatest thing I can do for you is to *be* as He is. It is in the *being* that releases the power of the Kingdom of Heaven, which enables us to see. In this place of *being*, sickness, disease, demonic entities, financial problems, emotional problems, relational problems, and the like cannot overcome your faith. Those things will have to get in line with who *you are*, or leave!

It is impossible to fail when you live in Christ. When you are *being*, you are being empowered constantly. God's grace to you cannot be overcome. His healing power cannot be overcome, and you do not even have to be conscious of these things. Your consciousness is free to plan for the future God reveals to you. Seek first the Kingdom of God, and His righteousness, and all the things will be added to you (Matthew 6:33). What things? Whatever you desire! When *you are* in Him, *you are* blessed by *I AM*. Because *He is*, you are. If He was not, you would not *be* either, but *He is* at the right hand of the Father now, and as *He is*, so are we in this world. Jesus said, *"I say to you, before Abraham was, I AM!"* (John 8:58). I say to you, before I was in my mother's womb, I am who He said I am. If the life I now live is Christ, I can say the life I now live is *I am*. This is where God is calling us to, but it is not a future destination, rather a present reality separated by the veil of fallen perception. When our perception is in the awareness of Christ Himself, we step into being.

The reality most of us live in is that we do not believe this reality exists today. It is true that everything in this world's system, and the demonic forces that drive it, would lead anyone to not believe what I have described. However, this does not mean that it cannot be done. We have to decide to let God be true, and every man be a liar. Before you can believe in God, you have to first believe there is a God. Before you can live in the reality of God, you first have to believe this reality exists.

How many people would drive their car from Los Angeles to New York City if they did not believe New York was going to be there when they arrived? It is the same in the realm of the spirit. There are spiritual realities that exist, no matter what we experience on the way to that reality. On our journey, we will be humbled by the resistance of the enemy through life experiences. If you have lived as a Christian for any period of time, you should already know this. When we become the embodiment of I AM, the Kingdom of Heaven will be seen in this world.

So, to be or not to be—that is the question. Jesus is the answer to the possibility of whether or not we can *be* as *He is*. So, again, who are you? When we stand before Jesus, He will know our *being!* I do not want to *be* someone He never knew. I want to hear, "Well done, good and faithful servant," and I want you to hear the same. Even in our name as people, we are called human *beings*. It is in the *being* of the Word that we become doers. If we are doing without *being*, our works are dead. It is impossible to have the *being* of Christ without the *doing* being made manifest. We have often heard our spirits described as our innermost *being*. If you are born again, you have to live in the *being* of what is innermost, and that is the new creation in Christ. When we live there, we are in a constant state of blessing and revival. To be in revival is to live in the *being* that is constantly *being* renewed daily. Scripture says we should *be being* filled with the Holy Spirit.

> *And the disciples were* **continually filled** *with joy and with the Holy Spirit.*
>
> ~ Acts 13:52 (emphasis added)

To be continually filled with the Holy Spirit and joy constantly occurs in the reality of *I AM*. When we speak *from* the I AM, we speak *for* the I AM. When *our will* is *His will, we are* as *He is*. If we want to be His messengers, we must also *be* the embodiment of the message. When *we are*, we will not only speak His will, but His will should also be felt tangibly by the hearer. We will emit the life force of His words. When Jesus told me that He was not mad at me, I absolutely knew it to be true because I experienced the reality of His love and feelings toward me. I received an impartation from what He said. It undid the powers of darkness and they fell to nothing in the presence of the Word Himself. That is why we must contend for His presence and be His presence to everything and everyone around us. All creation is groaning for this *reality of being* to take place within the sons of God.

The marriage of our lives, being the life of God, and our natural lives creates a totally unique expression of who God can be in the earth. It is God's unique idea of us as individuals that gives so much life to who God is in the earth. When we give our lives to Him, He increases His life to us. Your desires were given to you by God. I am not talking about perverse desires; I am talking about whatever is good and pure. You may be a journalist, a musician, a minister, a waitress, or an athlete, but you are far more than that. When any natural role is fulfilled by I AM, you are a world changer. God wants you to fulfill your dreams. He does not want you to be anything more than who you are in Him. If you are a professional fisherman, and you love doing that, then God wants you to continue to love doing that. He just wants to go fishing with you. Do not worship fishing—worship God only, and you will enjoy fishing like never before. God came to set us free and add His abundant life to us, not take life from us. The enemy and those who run with him are the ones who come to kill, steal, and destroy.

PERSECUTIONS

It was Jesus being I AM that caused the great healings and miracles. It was also what made the religious-spirited men want to stone Him. People who struggle with envy, jealousy, covetousness, arrogance, pride, etc., will not like anyone who speaks from this place of being. It will be a rock of offense that they will stumble over. There is no way around this reality, but it is a necessary reality that has to happen.

> *Jesus said, "Truly I say to you, there is no one who has left house or brothers or sisters or mother or father or children or farms, for My sake and*

for the gospel's sake, but that he will receive a hundred times as much now in the present age, houses and brothers and sisters and mothers and children and farms, **along with persecutions;** *and in the age to come, eternal life."*

~ Mark 10:29–30 (emphasis added)

We are mightily blessed when we forsake all for Jesus, but we will also experience persecution. The worst of the persecution will come from those you thought were your friends, but there are other types. Persecution comes from the demonic realm—even if it is manifested in men's hearts, its origins are from the demonic realm. Sickness, disease, mental illness, undue fatigue, trauma, unexpected death, crime, violence, hatred, accusation, racism, religious spirits, political spirits, unfaithfulness, hard-heartedness, anger, wrath, envy, coveting, jealousies, injustice, perverse spirits, lust, murderous spirits, lack, spirits of poverty, and the like will try to come and dethrone the Lord in your heart.

HEAVEN TO EARTH

However, Jesus said that on His foundation the gates of hell would not prevail. When you step out into your *being* of *I AM*, you will bring down Heaven to earth, but you will raise hell also! Everywhere Jesus went, demons would manifest. We as believers get the privilege of watching the Kingdom of Heaven collide with the gates of hell. When this happens, the earth trembles, and captives are set free of any and all bondages. Those who will, *will be*, and those who will not will be angry or sad.

Every great minister you can name has enemies who attack them with a vengeance. If you type in the name of a great minister who is impacting the world on an internet search engine, you will see written attacks against their ministry. The persecution is sometimes from those who claim to be ministers themselves. Those are usually the ones with hate in their hearts, who would probably be glad to see them gone at any cost. Those assaults are planned by demonic forces for the purpose of beating up those called by God. We do not fight against flesh and blood, however, and I will make no apology for beating the stew out of the demonic mindsets that some men walk in. Those structures need to be torn down and replaced with the mind of Christ.

> *The Lord's bond-servant must not be quarrelsome, but be kind to all, able to teach, patient when wronged, with gentleness correcting those who are in opposition, if perhaps God may grant them repentance, leading to the knowledge of the truth, and they may come to their senses and escape from the snare of the devil, having been held captive by him to do his will.*

> ~ 2 Timothy 2:24–26

To those men, we as ministers have to treat them in humility, correcting them if we are given the opportunity. This Scripture describes them as being taken captive by the enemy to do His will. If God opens up the opportunity, it should be taken. But I will tell you now, do not debate with a devil. Some men like to hash out things for the sake of looking spiritual and establishing their own dominance. When they are of this mind, they are speaking empowered by either a devil or their own ignorance. If it is a devil, you have to change your tactics according to what the Spirit of God says. But as a rule, do not waste your time trying to convince a devil of error. If the man who is influenced by the devil can hear you, talk to him, but do not give the devil a platform. Jesus told some of the Jews and Pharisees when they approached Him with their attacks that they were of their father, the devil! He did not spend His time speaking to them. Instead, He spoke to those who recognized who He was and submitted their ears to hear Him.

CHAPTER 14

Two Kingdoms

Obviously in this world there are many kingdoms; however, in the invisible realm, there are essentially two kingdoms: the Kingdom of God, which is light, and the kingdom of darkness. The Kingdom of God brings life according to the Tree of Life. The kingdom of darkness gets its wisdom from the father of lies, who uses the Tree of the Knowledge of Good and Evil to perpetuate his kingdom. As men and women, we are either living and moving in the Kingdom of light, or we are celebrated, dominated, or imprisoned by the kingdom of darkness. It is that simple. The delusion for those bound to the kingdom of darkness is that most of them live under the self-deception that they are free. The ones who know they are not free are simply dominated and imprisoned by the oppression of that kingdom. The kingdom of darkness seems good to most of those who are wealthy, powerful, beautiful, noble, and who have need of nothing.

Just because someone fits in one of those categories does not necessarily mean they are of the kingdom of darkness. It is the wisdom of this age that creates for example, pop culture and stars. It gives justice to those it approves and murder to those it disapproves. It is ruthless and greedy, and every form of evil that exists is born from it. Many Christians are bound by this kingdom, and some have been taken captive to do the will of its father.

The Kingdom of light, God's Kingdom, does not call many wise or noble. It qualifies those who have been rejected by men. It produces water in a dry and thirsty land. It came to Earth on behalf of the sick and dying. It came for the downtrodden and the brokenhearted, to find those who are lost and to give sight to those who are blind, to open deaf ears and make the lame walk. It came to earth to set free those who have been imprisoned. It came to give life to the lifeless, and resurrect the hearts of those who have been crushed. It came to Earth to deliver those oppressed by devils and fill them with the spirit of life, to restore the prodigal sons and daughters and lift up those who are lowly and meek, to give good news to the poor and restore their hope. It came to make peacemakers into sons and wield its sword against the injustices of evil. It came first as the Son of God, Love Himself! It is here now for eternity. The kingdom of darkness now begins to fade, and the Kingdom of Heaven increases with great intensity. The tides of this earth are changing and shifting to make way for the coming of the Lord. All creation is groaning for the manifestations of the sons of God!

We must now decide whom we are going to serve. Now is the time to draw the line in the sand. It will even be better for those who cannot draw the line presently, if we are willing to anyway. It is the heart of God to establish His Kingdom, our Kingdom, in the hearts of those who have become hopeless. We must be willing to pay the price of losing our lives to find His life, which cannot be purchased. God's Kingdom is not for sale. His word is not for sale. He cannot be bought, and those who live in Him cannot be bought. They have already been bought by the blood of the Lamb of God! They are the innocent ones who speak according to what they hear. They are the virgins who keep their wicks trimmed and patiently wait for their lover. They no longer are imprisoned by guilt or shame in their consciences, but they fully understand its ravages in others and do not rest until they set those free. It is the wisdom of our King to make the guilty innocent again. Would you be made whole? Would you decide to live in Him in spite of yourself and the contradictions that surround you? He chooses to live in you in spite of those things. Would you be free from the burden of your sin? There is power in the name of Jesus! There is power in the blood of Jesus!

For me personally, writing this book is the greatest miracle, besides being born again, that I have ever experienced. It is not that writing the book in itself is great; it is that God chose me to do it while remaining physically in one of the worst seasons of my life. At the beginning of the worst of this season, I wanted to die. Not only did I want to die at times, but I prayed that God would take me. Now, after several years, not only do I live, but I effectively live in Christ. And He, for His own good pleasure, decided to do an exploit while I still live in very adverse conditions. These conditions are no longer relevant to me, because I no longer see them or experience them in the same way. I can tell you from my experience as a deputy sheriff that men have killed themselves over a lot less pressure in one day than what I have had to endure for years. In fact, many have taken their own lives when they could only see the situation coming.

GLORIFY MY GOD

I do not speak this way to glorify myself; I say these things to glorify my God, because He alone gets the credit for what He has done in my life and the lives of my family. He sustained me when I couldn't take it anymore. He sustained me when I was having nervous breakdowns. He sustained me when I had nothing. He spoke to me even when I was drinking. He spoke to me when I was on antidepressants and no one else wanted to talk to me. He never left me or forsook me. So how could I dare boast in myself? I can boast in my weaknesses, and I can boast in His strength! He is glorious, and He deserves my praise. If someone doesn't understand where I'm coming from, it's only because they do not know what He has brought me through.

Everything I have written in this book, you can have working in your life, immediately. I live in the reality of the Kingdom of Heaven, and I boast in Christ—not myself—because I know where I was at the beginning of this season, and I know where I am now. The miracle is that I can write these things to you from a clear conscience, knowing that I speak the truth from the freedom I am experiencing right now. My wife and children have seen me transform right in front of their eyes. Over the past ten years, they saw me fall from grace only to return more determined than ever to live for God. They know and have seen this miracle transpire.

Some of you may have already said, "This guy must be an apostle, or this guy must be a prophet," etc. But what if I'm just a guy who found himself drowning in an ocean one day, and I realized that I was going to either sink or have to learn to swim? What if the Lord picked me up out of the water and taught me how to walk on this stormy ocean I found myself immersed in? What if I am just a guy who decided I didn't want to go out this way? What if God really did work all things together for my good because He knew that I loved Him and was called according to His purpose? What if He orchestrated the pressure Himself, so that a diamond could be formed?

If you are going to follow God, then you are going to have to trust Him—but I promise you that He can be trusted! If I am not the man I just described, does anything else about me really matter? Because everything that is added to me must be built upon the foundation of my living and moving and having my being in Him. What if I'm just a guy who has been, and is being, equipped? I do not believe you have to be apostolic or a prophet to hear God's voice. The whole point of having apostles and prophets is so the saints can walk in what they release. So, if they give it to me, is it not mine also?

REVELATION OF GOD'S GRACE

It is this revelation of God's grace that I no longer live but Christ lives in me that everything I do will be built upon. From this point on, I will live from this place. My hope, my faith, my love, and all of my gifts and callings are built upon this revelation: the revelation of reformation! I told my wife Christy that I didn't know if I was writing this book, or if this book was somehow writing me. For me, it is finished in the Spirit, and I will not be in these circumstances much longer. It was good for me to have this experience in Christ because He has shown me another level of His glory that I have only read or heard about before. So, I am no longer ashamed of what brought me to this place, but I am thankful that He did not fail me when I was failing myself. I tell you all these things because many of you feel like you have been living in a pit, or buried in a grave. The news I want to tell you is that, even in this place, you will know the power of His resurrection. You will find this place to be the catalyst that makes you fly.

I want to talk a moment about Dr. Kenneth Hagin's testimony. There is something that stands out about his testimony over most of what I have ever heard. When he was a teenage boy, he had three incurable diseases. Any of the three, as he was told by doctors, was ultimately going to kill him at a young age. Many of you have heard his testimony of being in the house in McKinney, Texas, where he was bedridden and dying from his conditions. He read in his grandmother's Methodist Bible:

> "Truly I say to you, whoever says to this mountain, 'Be taken up and cast into the sea,' and does not doubt in his heart, but believes that what he says is going to happen, it will be granted him. Therefore I say to you, all things for which you pray and ask, believe that you have received them, and they will be granted you."

> ~ Mark 11:23–24

He was just a young teenager when he read this Scripture and began to stand on it. But what separates his story is what he had to endure, not only from the sicknesses but from everyone else's doubt and unbelief. Not one person that I can recall said anything to help his faith. When preachers did come by to see him, all they would say was, "Don't worry, son. It will all be over soon." With friends like that, you don't need enemies! No one stood with him. He was alone with God as a boy, standing on the word of God. He would ask the visiting ministers, "What about this Scripture in Mark 11:23-24?" They would say that it is no longer for today. He could not get agreement from anyone.

It is one thing to overcome sickness with a church of believers agreeing that Scripture is true. It is another thing altogether to overcome sickness at that level when every other person in your life is full of doubt and unbelief! That took more true grit than most anything I have ever heard. We hear about Jesus performing miracles and healing, but we don't understand that He also stood alone. In some churches, if someone is sick, they will establish prayer teams, and great lengths are taken to assist the person who is sick. But Kenneth Hagin received his healing when he was alone and had not one ounce of encouragement from anyone. In fact, he was loaded down with everyone's discouragement. In spite of all that, he actually died and came back into his body before he was raised up healed. From that point on, he built his ministry from the revelation of Mark 11:23–24. He established Rhema Bible Institute in Tulsa, Oklahoma, and restored the message of faith back into the church, who had long since walked away from it. He brought faith back to unbelieving believers.

When Dr. Hagin was healed, it due to his faith in God's word which he held onto within his heart, and confessed out of his mouth. What was established in him spoke out and called those to himself that he would later instruct in his school. After a time, though, even in the greatest of places, the bad leaven comes to try and destroy what God is building. And this is not just in Hagin's ministry, but every ministry. People begin to feel elite in their own thinking, and they begin to sow their leaven into the house and it creeps through the fold. The enemy is then able to try to discredit a ministry, which was started by a boy who refused to doubt.

We'd better be careful how we look at and how we speak of other ministries, because when we do, God may remember the little boy that would not doubt Him, and I wouldn't want to have that anger directed at me. To God, we are not speaking against a ministry; we are speaking against His sons and daughters who went through hell and high water, believing the impossible. Even more than that, He remembers His Son who paid an enormous price for those who believe on Him. As far as I know, Rhema Bible Institute is doing just fine because I know it was built on the word of God.

TURN THEIR HEARTS TO GOD

Everyone who is going through the calamities of this life, where their very existence is being challenged, can turn their hearts to God. When you are determined to do that, He will speak to you just what you need to hear to change the situation. What He gives you during that season will be your foundation for the next season. It is during these times that you learn to live in Christ. The Foo Fighters had a song called "In Times Like

These" that I once had as my cellphone's ring tone. The chorus says, "In times like these we learn to live again. In times like these we learn to love again." When I was going through my worst, every time my phone rang, I heard those words. It was my reminder that these times are teaching me something. It is in these seasons of life where we learn the most important life lessons by experience.

I do not want this paragraph to get you out of the flow of what I have been speaking on, but I want to address what I perceive in my spirit. I can hear some of you now, saying, "Hey, that's a secular band; what are you doing listening to them?" They are a secular band, and at that time, they were the ones who were saying what I needed to hear. If a Christian artist had been saying what I needed, I would have listened to them! I am sure I do not agree with everything the Foo Fighters have written, but I don't agree with everything some Christian artists write and sing either. I can't wait for the day when we can all speak freely without having to qualify everything we say to appease the suspicions of men's hearts. That is from the leaven of the Pharisees. We have to look at each other after the spirit, and not after the flesh. When I listen to Bob Dylan, I can hear a prophet—others hear the devil. I choose to see an army when others choose to see dry bones. Ezekiel prophesied life into the dry bones because God saw an army. Ezekiel prophesied, and he saw the bones come together with ligament and sinew. Then he saw muscle and then flesh cover the bones, and he raised up an army (Ezekiel 37:1–14). You can't raise up what you are critical and suspicious of. If you are afraid of the dry bones, how will you raise them up? Who will speak to them and see them in the way God sees them? To the pure, all things are pure. To the defiled, even their hearts and consciences are defiled.

ASSUMPTION IS NOT DISCERNMENT

When it comes to standing on what God is showing you, this one thing I know: you will not always have a lot of encouragement from others because most people speak to you from the judgments they have already made about you. If what they speak is not from their judgments of you, it is from their own perceptions of life. In either case, it is not a lot of help, if any at all. For example, anything you do in life, those around you assume they know the reasoning for what you do. If you leave a church, some people will assume that you are either rebellious or offended. Then when you see one of those people, they will speak to you according to what they believe you are struggling with. That is because people feel their need to put everything into the box of their own perception. When we do that, we release death over people by speaking from a fallen perception. Assumption is not discernment. If you do not know why a person does what they do, do not assume according to your speculation. If the spirit of the Lord gives you something for that person, give it. Anything else in the name of your own fallen perceptions is from the evil one.

If you are called into an office of ministry, you will probably endure some hardships, but those He calls He equips, so it works out the same for all of us. I only say that so you are not discouraged by what you may endure. But if you have any mission of greatness, God will prepare you through the very thing that appears to be what comes to stop or kill your destiny. If you keep your faith in God, and don't quit, then you will not fail. It is impossible to truly live and move and have your being in God and fail. It cannot be done. When you live in that place in Him, you are sentenced to abundant life for eternity! You can live in Him anywhere. You can do that on the football field, the red carpet of the Golden Globes, on the streets, in prison, in the music industry, in the political arenas, in retirement, on the job, and even, if possible, in your local church! It is unfortunate that many Christians cannot live and move freely in their churches. Often, they are not even allowed to speak what God is doing for them in their local body. In some cases, it is far easier to follow the wind of the spirit when you are not in your local church. However, as tempting as it is to see dry bones, we must continue to see an army—particularly in the church.

As much as God hates injustice, He is a master at using it to establish in us the greatness to which He has called us. It is right to point out injustice when we see it, but even injustice cannot stop God. It will prove in the end to have been used only as a tool of instruction for His children.

The leaven of the Pharisees brings suspicion and elitism that is rooted in their own pride and entitlement. It is self-righteous in nature. This leaven of Herod is a corrupt kingdom or political system that is also rooted in pride. But it is most easily seen when it causes envy and jealousies since it then produces rivalries or competition between saints. This leaven has many other attributes that manifest as well, but suspicion, envy, jealousy, and rivalry are particularly causing most of the division that we experience in the church. Obviously, unbridled lust and greed are agents that can also bring division, but in those who have overcome the most obvious things of the flesh, they still sometimes struggle with the leaven of the Pharisees and Herod. That leaven creeps into everything and everyone. It not only divides churches, it divides marriages, and even individuals from within. The goodness of God rebuilds from within and it pulls together those who are called by His name.

FASTER AND FARTHER YOU WILL FLY

I heard T.D. Jakes on television the other night. He was talking about the pressures of life that people are enduring. He said that everyone holds greatness within themselves, and he revealed that we must learn to see ourselves as arrows in a bow. He explained that the weights and pressures of our lives are pushing the string of the bow further and further back, but God is the one holding the bow! As the pressure gets to the point where it no longer has the strength to hold you back any longer, it releases the string on the bow you are attached to. When that happens, you are released into your destiny, flying like an arrow. The harder and more intense the pressure, the faster and farther you will fly. That is how God actually uses the enemy to help launch you into your destiny. The strategies of the enemy can only propel you into your destiny. That's good news! That is the Gospel!

My hope is that you never hear me speak against anyone who is trying with all his heart to follow God. Being imperfect in your pursuit of God doesn't disqualify you. I do not speak against those, but I will not tolerate those who have given themselves over to the distorted perception Jesus died to set them free from. They speak in the name of the Lord as if they have a present revelation of Jesus, but they do not. These people serve Him with their lips, but their hearts are far from Him. They are filled with bitterness, anger, frustration, and the like— even if they boast in their ability to not walk in what the world calls sin.

They hold people hostage and only want to give to a person who sells their own souls to follow them. There is a big difference between those who know they don't have all the answers, yet they follow God with all their hearts, and the others I just described.

You have heard me give the words *assume* and *assumption* a real beating in this book. I did that because we cannot assume we know Jesus and His will; we must now know Him. What Jesus said is true about you and where you live, and you must *assume* the position of sonship because you *know* you are a son or daughter of His Father! You must know that, when He tells you He started a work in you, He will finish it! You must know that you can live in Him because He told you that you could. You can go ahead and *assume* you are going to have a glorious future only if you *know* it by His word. When you live in Him, you can *assume* all things are possible, but it must be transformed into *knowing* all things are possible! You can *assume* Jesus is trustworthy, and a friend that sticks closer than a brother, but you must *know* Him that way! When you live according to grace, *assume* that position, because your assumption is now based on Who you *know*. When you *know*, your *assumption* is based on Him who you *know*! However, do not *assume* you *know* Him. You must know that you *know* Him. Do not *assume* I am speaking the truth—you must *know* that it is the truth! We must not say we know; we must know by the spirit. We must recognize Jesus when we see Him, because the Holy Spirit in us knows who He is!

CHAPTER 15

The Mother of All Delusions

The mother of all delusions can also be defined as the 'ism' of all 'isms.' It is a form of pride, and it affects individuals as well as corporate entities. It is not exclusive to the church; it is found in every group of men who gather. It is the motivating power of all evil leaven that comes from any and all groups. It causes the division that the king of darkness prides himself in. It is subtle in its approach, and none will admit it. In fact, once someone is given over to it, he can hardly be brought to a place of truth again. It is a most serious negative condition that the people of God can be imprisoned by, and it is the power of the antichrist. It is the driving force of the wisdom of this age. It is called elitism.

Elitism creates an exclusive breed of man. It is kingdom-minded—it is just not of the Kingdom of Heaven. Every group of people who makes their allegiance with an ideology over the wisdom of God walks in elitism. It produces its own royalty. The elite of these elite groups are the nobility within these groups. They have a kingdom unto themselves; no other groups hold relevance unless they are of a kindred spirit. Education, political parties, corporations, science, engineering, religion, medicine, philosophy, art, pop culture, music, film, sports, journalism, capitalism, communism, socialism, fascism, racism, narcissism, anarchism, atheism, agnosticism, and sometimes even patriotism are all types of groups where elitism is found. It is not limited to the groups described, and, worst of all, it can be found in the church.

The leaven of the Pharisees found its power in elitism. The Pharisees had become a kingdom of elitists, and if you were not of their circles, you were substandard, particularly when it came to the things of God. They believed that they were the chosen of God to establish His way in the earth. Any other ideas of God from any others were deemed irrelevant, or, as in the case of Jesus, blasphemies. When Jesus arrived on the scene, they could not recognize Him because they themselves were delusional. It was their sense of being right that blinded them to truth and life.

There is no one more dangerous to other men than a delusional man who thinks he is right. Even within education, there are philosophical differences between educators. In political parties, you see the same. Most of these opposing philosophies view each other as the enemy of what they believe. However, the real enemy to each is the delusion that drives them. Elitism is a principality that drives each opposing group; so, essentially, one principality turns two opposing groups against each other! It is like the bully in the schoolyard who provokes two others to fight. He stands between them and says, "Let the best man spit on my hand."

When the one spits, he removes his hand so that the spit goes onto the other guy. Then he sits back and enjoys the fight! When this age is over, and we see the truth, we will be embarrassed by this.

Racism is a great example of this truth. One principality is the driving force behind the hate of two opposing races. It does not mean that real injustices are not done, but for someone to commit an injustice against another, they must believe they are entitled to commit it. In other words, they feel justified in their injustice. When a man feels justified by his delusion, he is dangerous! This is why Jesus warned us about the leaven of the Pharisees and the leaven of Herod. The only thing about the leaven of Herod is that it exists in every kingdom—the pop culture kingdom, the medical kingdom, the educational kingdom, the political kingdom, the music kingdom, the film kingdom. Do you get the picture?

Every kingdom has its leaven, and each kingdom chooses who it blesses or curses. Each kingdom has its own set of nobles and champions who are anointed by their kingdom to represent it, speak for it, and lead it. It is this way in the world, and sometimes it is this way in the church. Presently, the church sometimes has its own nobles. The church can have its own pop culture. We can create idols out of some leaders. I want to believe this is rare, but sometimes, we are a fad-driven society. The nobles of these kingdoms also believe they know better what you need than you do. They are usually very condescending towards anyone who thinks differently than them.

This is not to say that there are not Christians who have risen to the top of some of these kingdoms without compromising who they are. God loves when one of His children does that. That is the goal for some in the Kingdom of God. Tim Tebow and Tyler Perry, among others, are examples of some who have risen to a place of fame in a worldly kingdom. Those who are called for these platforms really need our prayers, not our jealousies. They are in a place where temptation would be unbelievable and overwhelming for some of us. So, what should be the difference between the kingdoms of this world and the Kingdom of God?

WE ARE CITIZENS OF HEAVEN

The kingdoms of this world are built on the ideologies of a fallen perception. Those who walk in these types of ideologies, in the sense that they are given over to it, are prideful in nature. You can be in one of these kingdoms vocationally and not be of its wisdom. In fact, we are all in these kingdoms at one time or another, but we are citizens of Heaven, not the kingdoms of this earth. If those who are given over to the systems they thrive in attempt to look humble, it will be false humility. If you do not believe me, then cross one of them, and you will see another side of their face, whether it be in the world or the church! Everyone can appear to be nice until they are crossed; then they cannot withhold their wrath because it is who they are.

The Kingdom of Heaven is built on our communion with the King of all kings. It is found in the place of true humility. It is found by men who know they are a mess and are in need of God's grace. Christian ideology is based upon the hearing of God's voice and the experience of His presence, the experience of God's love and power. It is the idea that Jesus himself is the Way, the Truth, and the Life, and those who find His life must lay down theirs. It is not a religion, but a relational position in the King Himself. He chooses whom He chooses, and He says He does not choose many nobles. Our King qualifies the disqualified and raises up the lowly in heart. He is the Alpha and the Omega, and we live, move, and have our being in Him. He is not a methodology but the living triune being! His ways are for the humble in heart. He does not debate with demonic principalities. He is holy. He is true.

It is true that some local churches can walk in the same delusion as any other kingdom if they come to the place where they believe they have "arrived." Pride is subtle and very blinding. We are no different than any other ideology if we do not remain humble in heart. We must walk in the spiritual wholeness of I AM. We cannot allow ourselves to be given over to elitism, nor can we stop it, unless we bow low in our hearts and remain a novice before our King. All men who have been given a great level of revelation from God will be tempted by elitism. If they say they are not, they are lying to you. We must all know from the beginning that elitism will be an enemy to us personally and to the Kingdom of God corporately. It is when we do not believe it is possible that we have already stepped off the cliff. Believe me when I say this. When we begin to believe our own press about ourselves, we are vulnerable. When we begin to love the flattery, we are vulnerable. When we finally get the acceptance we have longed for all of our lives, we are vulnerable. Even when we experience the deep love of God, we must be careful how we look at ourselves. Believe me—God does want us to think highly of ourselves, just not more highly than we ought.

When we get proud of how much we tithe, we are vulnerable. When we love the revelation more than the God of the revelation, we are vulnerable. When we love who we are in Him more than who He is in us, we are vulnerable. When we love to drop names, we are vulnerable. When we love our authority more than the ones we have authority over, we have already stepped off the cliff. Elitism is subtle, and when we are confessing our sins to one another, we had better consider adding this one to the mix. That is the way to defeat it. If you are not afraid to admit your temptation to elitism, then it will not have nearly the power it would if you will not admit it.

THE TEMPTATIONS OF ELITISM

I have fallen to elitism before; that is why I feel that it is necessary to talk about it now. I have been both the victim and the initiator of its wrath. Even the revelation God has given me in the writing of this book can tempt me to fall into the wisdom of this age. That is why it is important that I say these things. I will no longer refuse to admit my humanity just to be accepted by my peers. It is okay to desire the favor of your peers, as long as you do not worship the adoration of them. This is where the word subtle comes into play. I admit to the temptations of elitism so that I do not fall prey to them. If you truly want to be the man that God has called you to be, you must not be afraid of telling your weaknesses to others. I fear God, not how weak I may look before men.

If you fall prey to this, God will allow you to be humbled, so that you learn the lessons of your willfully blind condition. This is an act of God's love to you, should this happen. If we pray that we be humble, while we refuse the notion of our own existing pride, watch out! I know for a fact that, without the love of God in my life, I would be in a mess. It was those who were in a mess that recognized Jesus when He came—

not the elite, but the tax collectors, prostitutes, and blind. It was the blind who ended up seeing Jesus, not the ones who said they see. This is a paradox that we have to embrace in the Kingdom of God. I am a blind mess, yet I *am* he who is the voice of one crying in the wilderness.

When I was going through my pit experience, I listened to certain songs that I connected with during that time. Now, if I begin to think that I have arrived, I will listen to those songs again so that I remember clearly where I came from. When I hear those songs, the reality of the pit is ever so close. As long as I am willing to humble myself, He will exalt me. If I am unwilling, here I go again! I do not want to go around this mountain again.

Bob Dylan once wrote a song called, "You Gotta Serve Somebody." Nothing is more true. No matter who you are, you are serving somebody. If you think you are serving yourself, you are still serving somebody. You are essentially serving your own selfish ideology of who you believe you are. Some people serve the idea of freedom, and it has become an idol that empowers people to cast off restraint. Some people serve the notion of abstinence of any pleasures in life until they make this ideology an idol. Even our visions that come from God can become idols if they lead us to have a condescending attitude toward others' visions. We develop condescending hearts toward others when we are deceived into thinking *we* are the nobles of the Kingdom of God. Even if He has made you a noble, you should know that the greatest among you is the greatest servant, for the greatest is the one who lays down his nobility to serve. It is the one who lays down his nobility that receives the greatest nobility in the Kingdom of God. Even as I say these things, I sense my own lack in this area. Does this mean I am weak? Yes, but isn't that the reason Christ came? I would rather be weak and honest than blind and powerful.

Some people serve many ideologies. Some serve the Republican or Democrat ideologies, while some are serving the educational ideology. Some people serve the ideology of health gurus or even Kingdom principles. These scenarios could go on and on. As Christians, we do not serve ideologies; we serve the living God. As we hear, we speak; therefore, what we speak is true. We do not speak on our own, but we speak for Him who sent us. We know only Jesus and Him crucified, who now sits at the right hand of the Father in glory. Our knowledge is Him, not the idea of Him. When He reveals Himself to us in His glory, we are revealed with Him in glory (Colossians 3:4). Our unique individual desires, He Himself fulfills! We desire many unique things that are pure; in fact, in the words of Bill Johnson, we are God's idea. It is the marriage of who we are as individuals with Christ that is God's idea. The marriage of each individual with Christ reflects a unique glory and attribute of the King of kings Himself.

DOMINANCE AND SUBSERVIENCE

Those who are given over to their fallen perceptions normally walk in a dominant or subservient posture. Those who are noble dominate those who are subservient. It is the law of the jungle at work among men. It is from the evil one. This paradigm can be found in any kingdom of the world and sometimes in the church. There are men who cannot and will not have any relationship with other men unless they are ultimately the dominant presence in the relationship. They must see the other person bow to their ideology before they will walk any further with them. If you notice these types of men, look carefully at all of the relationships they have and see if this is not true. These types of men flatter you when they need you, ostracize you when they want your submission, and they will try to crush you to powder if you defy them. They can be businessmen, entertainers, apostles, pastors, husbands, or wives. They believe they increase when you decrease.

God is the Alpha and the Omega, He does not impose His will on those who *will not*. If you lose your life to find His, it is because you want to. He loves your choice in the matter so much that He will allow you to go to hell if you insist on it. Men are not that way. They will impose their will upon you if they can. They are cruel slave masters of their own ideology or desire, and there can only be one alpha among those. God wants all of His children to walk in the power of His attributes, and there is no one more alpha than the Alpha and Omega Himself! People who dominate others are weak bullies who are full of fear and insecurity, as well they should be.

Those who are of a subservient spirit are also walking in delusion. Subservience to an ideology, or methodology is the result of the fall, and it is nothing to be proud of. It is not humility; it is cowardice in nature, at the least—and it is an indictment that you do not know who you are and who you were created to be. God empowers and enables; He does not castrate your heart and will. God is not a thief who steals your peace and joy. He is not a bully who you must tiptoe around to avoid His wrath. He does not have to prove His authority; He is the King. Everything about Him releases the authority of who He is. He doesn't need cronies to satisfy His hunger and thirst for power; He is all-powerful. His heart is to empower the weak with His strength, not make them weaker. He does not bring up our faults all the time as if that would help us. He tells us who we are and how He loves us. His very presence reveals what we lack, and His goodness leads us to repentance.

SERVICE

The only true service that can come from a Christian is that which comes through knowing Christ Himself. If we are not living in the knowing of Christ, and we read that the greatest will be the greatest servant, we will set out on a quest to fulfill the role of a servant in a fallen perception. Even if the way we serve seems noble, it will prove in the end to be a dead work. The greatest service we can do for others is to be transformed into the image of Christ. When we are transformed into His image, by the intimate knowledge of who He is, our service will be perfected by design. Each one of us is a uniquely designed expression of Jesus Himself. It is the marriage of our will and His. When we serve from the place of our individual design, according to what He Himself has established in our hearts, we serve well.

If your ultimate service in life is to be a worship leader, yet you give yourself to so many other acts of service that you cannot possibly lead worship effectively, then you become a disservice to the Kingdom of God. Many people serve relentlessly to overcome the guilt of their stagnant condition. Many people are driven to serve the self-centered ambitions of those who say they are called. You could start orphanages, fight abortion, clean your local church, feed the poor, clothe the naked, and visit those in prison, but still not have revelation knowledge of Jesus.

As Arthur Burt says, it is not *what* you do but *why* you do what you do that matters.

When we live in Christ, there is a natural supernatural expression of love that will come from each believer specifically as he or she was baptized into the body of Christ. Whatever joint we are is how we are to serve. If my knee wants to act like my hand, I will be miserable because it does not have the grace to be a hand. It would also be a disservice to me if it tried. When my knee has the revelation that it is me, and it knows it has all the benefits of who I am, it will be satisfied, fruitful, and of great service to me. The knee being a part of my being has to be more important to my knee than its desire to be my hand. Our service must be from the overflow of who we are; then it will be satisfying for us, beneficial to man, and, more importantly, pleasing to God.

Service cannot be compartmentalized. We cannot think that sacrificial things are our only service. Being content with peace and joy is a great service to God and others. Excelling in our vocation is also a great service to the Kingdom of God. If we live in Christ, what else would we do?

God is raising up an army. He is raising up the least, the captives, and the outcast.

A WORD FROM THE LORD:
TO MY CHOICE ONES AND THEIR SCOFFERS

To you that I have chosen, be blessed and be still and know My love for you. Hear Me, and see Me as I AM. I love you, and My heart longs for you. I AM for you. I chose you and have come for you, My brokenhearted ones, My bruised ones, My blind ones, My deaf ones, My lame ones, My poor ones, My imprisoned ones, My weary ones, My weak ones, My meek ones, My sick ones, My oppressed ones, and all who are lowly of heart. I have personally come to give you good news. To proclaim My liberty to you. Not to condemn you, but to give you My abundant life, according to My riches in glory. I have come to qualify those who have been disqualified. I have come to renew life where the enemy has drained it. It is My pleasure to do this because My Father wants this, and My food is to do His will.

I AM decides who He will be merciful to, and I AM decides who He will not have mercy for, because I AM He who sits on the throne. I AM He who sits in the throne room of grace, and I AM who decides who receives My grace. If you choose to receive My grace, it is because I chose you to receive My grace even before you were in your mother's womb. Many will scoff and say I have no right to speak this way, but I AM the one who decides who has what rights, and who speaks what way because I AM He who sits on the throne. Where were they when I laid the foundations of the earth? I choose whom I choose based upon My good pleasure and My love. No one knows who I AM but that is not revealed to them, and I AM giving Myself to the least. I give Myself to those I chose to call My own, and I call the lowly of heart to exalt, and exalt I will! I AM He who is here to raise up the ruined. I AM He who respects the shamed and mends the broken. I AM the advocate of victims and the only hope for offenders.

I will raise up those who have been declared dead in heart to be the instructors of the living. I will release My imprisoned ones to teach My freedom. I will remove the sickness off of the oppressed, and they will be a wellspring of healing. My lame will walk, and the wise will be confounded. I will remove the oppression from those who grieve, and they will mourn no more. I will keep company with those who are lonely, and set them in families. I AM He who gives liberty to the captives; I AM He who sits on the throne. I AM He who will sit among My chosen, as a refiner's fire, and I will purge them of their iniquities. I will purify whom I will purify because I AM He who sits on the throne.

Even now as I say these things, you who accuse continue to scoff. Excuse Me, who did you say that you were? You who would remind and instruct Me, on the day of your judgment, of your great miracles and *prophecies—do I know you? For I say I never knew you, and you have your reward for what you have done. You call unclean what I have made clean. You call impure those I have made pure. You stalk the vulnerable and expose the weaknesses of My sheep. You need to pray that I would even grant you repentance, you arrogant ones. You enslave those who are already enslaved. You oppress those who are already oppressed. You steal from those who have already been robbed. You bruise those who have already been crushed. You make sicker those who are already sick. You place stumbling blocks in front of the blind, and you deafen the deaf with corruption. You cause the lame to trip, and the weak to fall. And somehow you do this in My name, and yet you have no shame. Who are you again? I came to destroy the works of the devil, and now I am having to destroy your works as well. You who capture the imprisoned have been taken captive yourself to do the will of the spiritual wickedness you walk in. Take the eye salve of Heaven so that you might see again, because you tread very closely to the doorway of the decided fate of the evil one and his entourage.*

We must change the way we see and do things, especially today if we desire to be leaders. We must learn to walk in love. God is releasing judgments on things that have been left alone at certain levels for centuries, but as the dispensation of grace increases, so too will His judgments on His people who do not relent in the way they have been walking. Even the injustices have been being used for this moment with extraordinary purpose. God uses all things for the good of those who love Him and are called according to His purpose (Romans 8:28). Blessed be the name of the Lord.

CHAPTER 16

The Great Pretenders

The world, and the church, is full of great pretenders. People are starving for genuine truth. It is the cry of our hearts. In the world we have pop culture, which presents a world that is larger than life. It is a world that does not see the others around it. It is predominately focused on itself. That is not to say that there are not great people who are in the limelight of that culture; I am speaking primarily of the heart of the culture itself. Some people love the lies of this world, and pop culture fulfills the need for that hunger. The world wants a star that will shine for them and fulfill their lust for the lie. It is a mystery, yet a reality, that exists in our culture here in the United States. This phenomenon is not only restricted to the United States, though. It is global in nature, particularly since technology has been upgraded to its current levels.

The lie presented is that this culture is how most people in our country live, but reality is far from the presentation. No wonder other countries who are in need despise us when they are exposed to our television and the internet. They see the red carpet and the glamour, the mansions, the movies, and the reality shows, which are far from reality. They see street gangs depicted on television, prostitution, pornography, Wall Street crooks, hardened criminals, supermodels, greed, and corruption. They see reality television shows that are a joke. They see idol worship of every kind and leave thinking, "Is this what the United States is all about?"

They do not see the everyday lives of ordinary Americans going to work, raising their families, washing their clothes, and saying grace at the dinner table. They do not see humility and neighborly love. They do not see the love that exists between family members. They see political agendas; they see a culture filled with sexual perversions, violence, lawlessness, gangs, organized crime, and the like. If you took one day of news and some of the shows available to anyone on television today, and went back in time and showed it to a group of people in the 1930s, I believe many would die of heart failure. They would not be able to wrap their brains around what they would see. Imagine what people in remote regions think when they get exposed to the culture that is presented on our televisions. They would see the great Satan, as some call us! However, we know, living here, that pop culture is not reality. You do know that, right? You do know that it is the entertainment industry, right? And the news, for the most part, only reports bad news. If you do not know these things, I feel it is my responsibility to tell you.

We as a people have become a culture that follows either pop culture or gang culture for relevance in how we should dress, think, and act. Unfortunately, as I have already touched on, we bring that same type of thinking right into the house of God. We also have our stars who can no longer see past the culture they have created for themselves. They only see each other. Their Christian pop culture may be their alliances, networks, or denominations. Their view of the Kingdom of Heaven is within their organization. In fact, some would not recognize their Master's voice in anyone not affiliated with their group. We cannot let this continue. Those who are in these circles of influence must rise up to stop this mentality. That does not mean that the alliances, networks, or denominations are evil in and of themselves. It is men and malevolent spirits who divide, and it is men who make denominations and alliances. So it will be men who need to see and hear what the Spirit is saying and make the appropriate changes in their hearts. This is a metaphorical circumcision that needs to happen in the church at a global level, particularly here in the United States.

As the church, we also sometimes present a culture that is unreal in its presentation. We present perfection, with our best men out front leading the way. We only talk about our strengths, and we speak from a platform of strength, as if we are not depending on the grace of God ourselves. We tell everyone to fake it until they make it, which is one of the worst statements we can propagate. We do not have to pretend we are perfect to stand in faith in our perfect God. He never intended that we would have to pretend to be something we are not. Who we are now is enough for God. If He could talk to a prophet through a mule, can't

He use us? If He could ride into Jerusalem on an ass's foal, are we not enough just like we are?

A RELIGIOUS BOAT

One of the reasons Jesus hung out with tax collectors and prostitutes was that they did not pretend to be anything other than who they were. The reason He chided the Pharisees and Jews was because they insinuated they were the chosen of God, who knew what He desired from men. But Jesus said they were whitewashed tombs who outwardly looked great, but inwardly they were full of dead men's bones (Matthew 23:27). That was the Jewish pop culture of that day. When we create an environment where people have to pretend, we create the same kind of culture—a culture where people are more mindful of fitting in and meeting our requirements than of being who they are. When we create an environment where people feel they have to pretend so that they do not rock the boat, we have created a religious boat!

Ministers should be preaching to those imprisoned by carnal living. Ministers must know that the same grace that enables them to preach is the same grace that allows the prisoners to come into the presence of the Lord. No one escapes their need for grace; if they tell you they do, they lie. The fact is that grace is required for everyone to function in the Kingdom of God, or no one could lawfully do anything. If we preach as though we ourselves do not need grace, then we lie. If we have an atmosphere where our knowledge, our works, and our order are more superior than His grace, then we lie. If we say our revelation is what enables us more than the revelation of His enabling grace, then we lie. If we say that grace is only to get you into the Kingdom and then you must learn His ways, apart from grace, we are not telling the truth. His grace is His way. Grace is the power that we were saved by and walk in. It is a foundational pillar of our existence in Him. It is what enables us to be established in and on Jesus, the rock of our salvation. It is His free gift to us. It is the gift of the Father's love to the world. If they will receive it, they will be changed, forever! Grace is the power that saves us and keeps us, and Jesus is the Lord of grace! We do not have to pretend we are in faith.

We are either in faith or we are not. Even when we are being tempted to believe we are pretending, we are not because our Kingdom and our Lord are real. We do not need to pretend, exaggerate, manipulate, or intimidate. All we need to do is marinate in His word and emulate! It is then that we come into the knowledge of the truth!

CHAPTER 17

Living in the Spirit

Now on the last day, the great day of the feast, Jesus stood and cried out, saying, "If anyone is thirsty, let him come to Me and drink. He who believes in Me, as the Scripture has said, out of his heart will flow rivers of living water." **But this He spoke concerning the Spirit, whom those believing in Him would receive***; for the Holy Spirit was not yet given, because Jesus was not yet glorified.*

~ John 7:37–39 (emphasis added)

When we talk about living in the Kingdom, we are talking about living in the reality of the eternal realm. To do this, we must live in the Spirit of God. Nothing in the Kingdom of God can be built or sustained without the involvement of the Holy Spirit. We are to live, move, and have our being in Christ. It is impossible to live in Christ without the involvement of the Holy Spirit. When we follow the Holy Spirit, we follow Christ, because the Holy Spirit does not speak of His own, He always leads us to

Christ. They are one in the same, as God. We are spirit, soul, and body. God is triune also. He is God the Father, God the Son, and God the Holy Spirit. The Holy Spirit is God, just as the Father is God, just as Jesus is God. Scripture says the fullness of the Godhead dwelled in Christ. Paul speaks concerning Jesus:

> *For in Him all the fullness of the Deity dwells in bodily form; and in Him you have been made complete, and He is the head over all rule and authority…*
>
> ~ Colossians 2:9–10

The Holy Spirit is the person of the Trinity who led Jesus throughout His entire ministry. It was through the power of the Holy Spirit that Jesus knew what He saw His Father doing, and what He heard His Father saying. Scripture says that Jesus laid down His Godly attributes and walked the earth as a man—but not just any man, a man empowered and endowed by the Holy Spirit.

> **Jesus, full of the Holy Spirit**, *returned from the Jordan* **and was led around by the Spirit** *into the wilderness for forty days, being tempted by the devil. And He ate nothing during those days, and when they had ended, He became hungry.*
>
> ~ Luke 4:1–2 (emphasis added)

There is nothing accomplished with any eternal value that does not require our participation with the Holy Spirit. When the disciples were hiding from the Jews, Jesus walked through the walls into the room where they were. He spoke with them concerning the Kingdom of God, and then He breathed on them, telling them to receive the Holy Spirit. At that point they were born again, but Jesus instructed them to do something else. He told them to go to Jerusalem and wait for the promise of His Father, which they had heard from Him. They were to wait in Jerusalem for the baptism of the Holy Spirit. Now that Jesus was glorified and was going to ascend to the Father, He was telling them that everything He had done on this earth was so that all men could have what He was commanding them to wait on in Jerusalem. It was not an option if they were going to follow Him; it was a requirement. He died for this moment in time when men could walk the earth as He did. He called men to walk in an invisible realm that would be made visible through their exploits. To do these things, it would require the Holy Spirit.

> *Gathering them together, He commanded them not to leave Jerusalem, but to wait for what the Father had promised, "Which," He said, "you have heard of from Me; for John baptized with water, but **you will be baptized with the Holy Spirit** not many days from now." So when they had come together, they were asking Him, saying, "Lord, is it at this time You are restoring the kingdom to Israel?" He said to them, "It is not for you to know times or epochs which the Father has fixed by His own authority; but you will receive power when the Holy Spirit has come upon you; and you shall be My witnesses both in Jerusalem, and in all Judea and Samaria, and even to the remotest part of the earth."*

~ Acts 1:4–8 (emphasis added)

So the disciples waited in Jerusalem as they were instructed. They numbered about one hundred and twenty, including the apostles of the Lamb. As they were waiting, they prayed and were in one accord. The rest is history, and I will let Scripture tell of the account:

When the Day of Pentecost had come, they were all together one place. And suddenly there came a sound from heaven a noise like a violent rushing wind, and it filled the whole house where they were sitting. And there appeared to them tongues as of fire distributing themselves, and they rested upon each one of them. And **they were all filled with the Holy Spirit** *and began to speak with other tongues, as the Spirit was giving them utterance.*

Now there were Jews living in Jerusalem, devout men from every nation under heaven. And when this sound occurred, the crowd came together, and were bewildered because each one of them was hearing them speak in his own language. They were amazed and astonished, saying, "Why, are not all these who are speaking Galileans? And how is it that we each hear them in our own language to which we were born? Parthians and Medes and Elamites, and residents of Mesopotamia, Judea and Cappadocia, Pontus and Asia, Phrygia and Pamphylia, Egypt and the districts of Libya around Cyrene, and visitors from Rome, both Jews and proselytes, Cretans and Arabs—we hear them in our own tongues speaking of the mighty deeds of God." And they all continued in amazement and great perplexity, saying to one another, "What does this mean?" But others were mocking and saying, "They are full of sweet wine."

~ Acts 2:1–13 (emphasis added)

Can you imagine the scene? It must have been incredible to witness such a thing. It also gives a description of how unbelievers may perceive the things of the Spirit. Some heard them speaking in their native tongue, while others saw men who were drunk with wine. Any time the Spirit of God is manifesting, that will always be the case. But Peter addresses the crowd with an extraordinary power and authority.

But Peter, taking his stand with the eleven, raised his voice and declared to them: "Men of Judea and all who live in Jerusalem, let this be known to you and give heed to my words. For these men are not drunk, as you

*suppose, for it is only the third hour of the day; but this is what was
spoken of throught the prophet Joel:*

*'And it shall be in the last days,' God says,
'That I will pour forth of My Spirit on all mankind;
And your sons and your daughters shall prophesy,
And your young men shall see visions,
And your old men shall dream dreams.
Even on My bondslaves, both men and women,
I will in those days pour forth of My Spirit
And they shall prophesy.
'And I will grant wonders in the sky above
And signs in the earth below:
Blood, and fire, and vapor of smoke.
'The sun will be turned into darkness,
And the moon into blood,
Before the great and glorious day of the Lord shall come.
'And it shall be that whoever calls on the name of the Lord will be saved.'"*

~ Acts 2:14–21

Peter went on to preach a lot more than this. When the people heard Peter, those who gladly received what he said were saved, and that was about three thousand people! Then Scripture says that fear came upon the hearts of every person, and many signs and wonders were done through the apostles. Another realm had imposed itself onto the followers of Jesus. That same eternal realm is here now for all of us who believe.

Jesus said that, if we abide in Him and His word, He would manifest Himself to us. If God is not manifesting Himself to us, then we have to ask ourselves, "What are we missing?" Jesus did not just come to save us from hell, but He came to live among us, and inhabit our lives! If Jesus is not manifesting to us and through us, we are just another group of people steeped in our own opinions. That is a religious-spirited people who live in their own opinions. Jesus did not call us to live in an opinion, but the very spirit of God. He wants us to be saturated and permeated with His presence. He wants us living in a realm that makes the natural realm here on earth consciously irrelevant. The Kingdom of Heaven is not relevant to this world, nor are the people of it. The wisdom of this age, and the people of that wisdom likewise, are not relevant to the Kingdom of Heaven. He wants all men to receive Him and become relevant. But when it comes to His Kingdom being established on the earth, no one nor anything has dominion over the power of it. His Kingdom is a superior kingdom. His heart is to subdue all other kingdoms so that they bow their knee to His.

For this to happen, we have to be elevated through transformation into who we are in Christ, through the renewing of our minds. Renewing our minds does not come through just reading Scripture. Renewing our minds comes from submitting ourselves to the processes of the spirit of God. Our renewal can and will come in many ways, including Scripture. All things will work together through this process of transformation for the good of those who love Him, and are called according to His purpose (Romans 8:28). Everything we encounter in this life will serve us in the transformation process, if we submit ourselves to God and the work of His Holy Spirit.

For all who are being led by the Spirit of God, these are sons of God.

~ Romans 8:14

But if you are led by the Spirit, you are not under the Law.

~ Galatians 5:18

If we have been filled with the Holy Spirit, then we will manifest the spirit. 1 Corinthians 12 lists nine manifestations, or gifts, given by the Holy Spirit.

Now there are varieties of gifts, but the same Spirit. And there are varities of ministries, and the same Lord. There are varieties of effects, but the same God who works all things in all persons. But to each one is given the manifestation of the Spirit for the common good. For to one is given the word of wisdom through the Spirit, and to another the word of knowledge according to the same Spirit; to another faith by the same Spirit, and to another gifts of healing by the same Spirit, to another the effecting of miracles, and to another prophecy, and to another the distinguishing of spirits, to another various kinds of tongues, and to another the interpretation of tongues. But one and the same Spirit works all these things, distributing to each one individually just as He wills.

~ 1 Corinthians 12:4–11

There is no question about it: if we are baptized with the Holy Spirit, we should be manifesting regularly the gifts of the spirit of God, because He wills it! I have heard people say that, if God wanted them to manifest a gift of the Spirit, such as speaking in tongues, they would speak in tongues. But if you applied that same logic to salvation, it is like saying, "If God wants me to be saved, then I will be saved." How many of you know that is not the way it works? When we became saved, we had to *ask* God to come into our lives. Then we had to *believe* and *use our faith to receive* the provision of our salvation.

The baptism of the Holy Spirit is no different. We must receive the Holy Spirit, fully knowing who we receive, and we will manifest His gifts as He wills, just as the Scripture says. To be honest, once we have heard the truth on this matter, it is usually our lack of humility coupled with doubt and unbelief which keeps us from receiving this free gift. I am convinced that is why He made it this way on purpose. The door of humility is always the doorway for us who believe. We do not like having to go through any door that we can't drive our Mercedes through. If you are born again, it is absolutely pivotal that you turn your heart to God and ask for the increase that comes through the Holy Spirit.

As great as the gifts of the Spirit are, the fruits of the Spirit are greater. The fruits of the Spirit are always the expression of Love Himself.

If I speak with the tongues of men and of angels, but do not have love, I have become a noisy gong or a clanging cymbal. If I have the gift of prophecy, and know all mysteries and all knowledge; and if I have all faith, so as to remove mountains, but do not have love, I am nothing. And if I give all my possessions to feed the poor, and if I surrender my body to be burned, but do not have love, it profits me nothing.

Love is patient, love is kind and is not jealous; love does not brag and is not arrogant, does not act unbecomingly; it does not seek its own, is not provoked, does not take into account a wrong suffered, does not rejoice in unrighteousness, but rejoices with the truth; bears all things, believes all things, hopes all things, endures all things.

Love never fails; but if there are gifts of prophecy, they will be done away; if there are tongues, they will cease; if there is knowledge, it will be done away. For we know in part and we prophesy in part; but when the perfect comes, the partial will be done away. When I was a child, I used to speak like a child, think like a child, reason like a child; when I became a man, I did away with childish things. For now we see in a mirror dimly,

242

but then face to face; now I know in part, but then I will know fully just as I also have been fully known. But now faith, hope, love, abide these three; but the greatest of these is love.

~ 1 Corinthians 13:1–13

But the fruit of the Spirit is love, joy, peace, patience, kindness, goodness, faithfulness, gentleness, self-control; against such things there is no law.

~ Galatians 5:22–23

If you are baptized in the Holy Spirit, you will manifest gifts and fruits. There are no laws against anything that the Spirit of God would ask you to do. There may be religious objections from pious men, but there are no laws against it. God has asked each one of us to believe in a virgin birth; the death, burial, and resurrection of our Savior; and now, on top of that, He wants us to be filled with His Spirit at a level where we manifest His gifts and bear His fruits. In this world, with all of its wisdom, that is insanity. So, if you want to please God, you must embrace the fact that He has called us to believe the unbelievable, to do the impossible. He prefers we be all-in or all-out. If you are not all in, at least be quiet so that you are not like the Pharisees Jesus chided. He told them they did not enter in, and they prevented others who were trying to enter from entering! Religious-spirited people always try to prevent others from entering the place God has designed for them.

From a historical overview, the Early Church walked in a large amount of God's glory. Since then, His presence has not been seen in the concentration that it was then. As the church was scattered, the former glory began to wane. This degrading lasted for hundreds of years. I believe the Dark Ages were the direct result of the waning light of the church. However, one man named Martin Luther got the revelation that we were saved by grace through faith, and an increasing of the light began to return in the earth.

Since that pivotal moment, the glory of God has incrementally increased at greater and greater levels. The Azusa Street Revival happened at the turn of the 20th century, and even more increase began to manifest. Each dispensation since then has added another level of glory and restoration. Throughout the 1900s, others rose up and imparted necessary truths of restoration. With each release, the proximity between outpourings and impartations of restoration has gotten closer and closer together. If you look at these great dispensations as birthing pains, you can easily see that the church is at hand to deliver something the world has not seen to date. I believe the time is now for this baby to be born, when the latter rain will be greater than the former rain! We were created for this moment in time!

The increase of His Kingdom cannot be separated from the workings of the Holy Spirit in our lives. The deeper we go in Him, the greater the manifestation of the gifts and fruits of His Kingdom. When we manifest the things of the Spirit, we manifest the Kingdom of Heaven.

CHAPTER 18

The Pit

In Chapter 1, I described to you the pit that I had fallen into. What I want to share in this chapter is how the Lord has delivered me and reformed me, even while I was in the pit. My hope is that this will be good news for everyone who has found themselves feeling helpless, formless, and void. I also hope that, if you have never been in this kind of situation, you can glean wisdom that will help you identify God's hand in your situation.

As I have shared already, I became aware of my call to ministry in 1997. I was excited about the opportunity to set out on a new adventure. I really did love God, and I loved people too. I loved the gathering together of the saints. I loved to feel God's presence during worship. I loved singing and playing, and I loved writing songs. I deeply loved experiencing God's anointing through ministers that I have heard. There was nothing about God that bothered me, and there was nothing of real measure that would bother me deeply about the church at large. I thought I was ready to go, and that I possessed everything I needed to accomplish my mission. What I did not know was how naïve I was about the devices of the enemy. I also did not have a revelation of what I thought was a strong foundation. As much as I thought I knew about life and standing up for truth, as a strong warrior, I found myself poor, miserable, blind, and naked.

I found myself in a place where I had no answers. The answers I was getting, mostly from others who thought they knew what I was going through, were like salt in open wounds. Some things you hear in a time like that, though it may come from Scripture, can release more death over you than you are already experiencing. The letter of the law kills, but the Spirit brings life (2 Corinthians 3:6). I did have encouragement from some. My brother Bill would say, "God is going to use this thing you're going through—you watch and see. I promise you there is far more going on here than you can see." That encouragement was one of the things said that helped me personally—one of those simple statements that compelled me to look for the positive possibilities that God really was working through this. Encouragement goes a long way, and, believe me, I was in need of courage.

I also listened to teaching CDs by different ministers, including Bill Johnson, Graham Cooke, and others that helped a lot. God was speaking to me, but I was in need of a resurrection—even though I was quite alive biologically.

I read several books during this time as well. It seemed like every book I picked up stressed that people with certain callings often have a pit experience. They would outline the story of Joseph's experience or Job's. I really could relate to that possibility, but how could I know that's what was happening to me? How could I be sure, because it didn't seem like Joseph or Job had done anything to deserve what they endured? Deep inside, I felt ashamed of the moral failure in my heart and fiscal bankruptcy that I had experienced. I thought I got what I deserved, that I was an unfaithful steward of all that God had asked of me, and I had let Him down. I also was deeply tested about believing whether I was good, or whether God was good. So, the bottom line was that I didn't think very highly of myself or God. I am just being real with you, and as transparent as I know to be.

So, here is a lesson: be honest with God and someone you can trust about what you are feeling in your heart—the good, the bad, and the ugly. That can be easier said than done. I didn't trust God the way I should, or anyone else for that matter. But those I had a measure of trust with, I did speak to. There were some I told what I was feeling and dealing with so I would know whether or not I could trust them. I really did not feel at the time that I had a lot more to lose. I know for a fact that some Christians cannot wrap their brains around other Christians finding themselves in a situation like I was in. The possibility just doesn't register. I also know that, unless you've been there, it's almost impossible for a Christian to have the understanding they need for someone in that condition. I know this—because I was one of them.

So what did I do? The first thing I had to do was reach a conclusion about God. Was God good? I knew deep down in my heart that He was, but I needed to see what was causing me to question His goodness. Why did I even have the question? Because I was angry with God. I set out for ministry to do His will, and all I got for it were trials, tribulations, betrayal, heartache, and destruction. I thought, "Not only am I mad at you, but I don't like anyone who calls themselves a minister, and I don't want to be counted among them. All they will do is use you and hurt you." That's some pretty harsh words for someone to say isn't it? That was what was in my heart. It was the fact that lightning had not struck me for what I said—that was the beginning of seeing God's goodness! My wife, Christy, would say, "Please don't stand near me when you make statements like that!" I do not blame her; it does prove God is longsuffering.

PRIDE SETS ITSELF UP AS AN OFFENSE TO GOD

So, I determined to trust God, even if I was battling bad thinking or not. God did begin to point out some things to me. I saw the large amount of pride that I walked in. It's hard to show a prideful person that they have been in pride. The nature of pride itself blinds you to this truth. You can be so prideful that you could never believe that it is you standing in the need of prayer. Plus, you think you are wise enough to argue with the notion and deny it. Pride sets itself up as an offense to God. It is everything that He is not. I had received the revelation of the prideful attitude in my life. I began to humble myself under the mighty hand of God. The problem with that is not being proud of finding refuge in humility because if you do that, it is no longer humility. The revelation was an event where I thought I got it, and I did by faith.

However, what still remained was the process that brings the revelation from Heaven to earth. At the time I got the revelation of pride, I had not yet filed bankruptcy. In fact, I was trying to maneuver and prevent that from happening. Somehow, I thought, because I had gotten a revelation on pride, I could go on with my life. I checked that off my to-do list and I thought for sure things would begin to fall into place. However, when I went through the bankruptcy, the impartation of revelation went into the beginning of the transformation mode. The humiliation allowed the transformational process plenty to work with. It is in the place of transformation where we grow up into our revelation. Could I have learned this any other way? Apparently, I could not. Many would argue that God would not allow those kinds of things to happen to His people, but they did happen to me. They have happened to a lot of Christians before me. Some would say that the favor of the Lord was removed from me, but I say I found the favor of the Lord that delivered me in this place, and it will deliver others in the same condition.

After the bankruptcy was when the mother lode fell upon me. It was the point of crushing. I was broken, and I was being crushed further into powder. Does everyone have to go through this kind of thing? Not everyone, but the fact remains that I went through it. Scripture says that Jesus learned obedience through His sufferings. Paul experienced sufferings, and so did Joseph, Job, Moses, and Peter. In fact, if we are honest, we all experience a measure of sufferings. Scripture says that we share in His sufferings (2 Corinthians 1:5-6). This world is full of suffering; that's why Jesus came in the first place. He gave us what we needed to go through all the adversities of life, whether they were self-inflicted or not. Business-wise, I don't know what I could have done that would have stopped what happened. Some things in my life I know were in my power to do differently, and some things came from external sources.

HIS SPIRIT WITHIN US

So, we can agree that some things can happen beyond our control, and some things happen that could have been different, had we chosen better. This I do know: God knows what is in our hearts. He doesn't test us so that He will know what's in us. He tests us so *we* will know what is in us! God is not surprised nearly as much as we are. He called us when we were yet sinners, so He knows what the process of transformation will be for each one individually. If we do not hunger and thirst for Him as we should, He knows just what it will take to get us hungry and thirsty. He is the author and perfecter of our faith, and He is a master builder in the things of life. We will see far better in the spirit, when we realize we are blind, than we ever will thinking we have the ability to see. Now, what He reveals to us, we see, but we only see because of His Spirit within us. When we lose our vision of God Himself in our lives, we are blind. Well, you might say, "He never leaves us." That's true, but if I have no vision, then I'm perishing. The bottom line: I was in a pit, and I lacked vision.

The hardest thing to realize when you are in this condition is where to direct your focus, because in that kind of place, you really do not even know what to focus on. When you are overwhelmed, the first thing you have to make yourself do is focus on God. You may not feel like it; you may even feel that you can't. There may be days you don't focus on God as you should, but do not quit. If you ultimately quit, you are through.

Keep going to a church where other believers are, if it is not too brutal on you. I found myself at a place where I had to make a choice. Was I going to lie down and die, or fight the best I could? Now, the best you can fight is between you and God, because while most people believe they know what your best should be, , more than likely they do not have a clue.

One thing that comes from being in a pit-type situation is that you learn to seek after and hear God's voice. You have to be determined that you are going to go after God even if it kills you, which is actually the goal, is it not? You will also learn to be obedient to God in this place. You will find your true identity in this place of relationship He is developing in you. It is that secret place between you and Him. God wants to develop a relationship that is so intimate and holy that some of your experience is just to be between you and Him. To go to this place, you have to go alone. When you return from this place, though, you return in power.

Because of the bankruptcy, physical ailments, mental illness, unemployment, depression, empty bank account, a backslidden condition, and the judgment and humiliation that came with all of it, I had to be determined to get my mind off of these things and onto what I knew was my only hope. When you are my age, in that kind of position, Jesus is the only hope. I decided to just ignore what I could not control or fix with my hands. I had to learn to reckon myself dead to sin and circumstances. It is not an easy thing to do, but it was absolutely a life and death decision and battle I had to make it through. After years of facing turmoil in this fight, I began to make steps, little by little, that brought more and more strength. Then one day I was listening to a

Damon Thompson CD entitled, "The Fight For Faith." The Lord really touched my heart and I began to weep, and I felt a sense of power to press further into God.

LEARNING TO STRENGTHEN MYSELF IN THE LORD

I felt like the Lord was showing me how to walk one step at a time. I had heard a Bill Johnson teaching about being focused on our problems instead of the answer—Jesus! So I determined that no matter what awful thing would present itself, I was going to turn my heart to God and listen to His word or listen to worship music. Sometimes I would read a book or the Bible. When a bill would come that had to be paid immediately and we had no money, I would put on a CD and just worship God. If we got behind on our rent and we were out of food, which happened almost every single month, I would seek the Lord all the harder. I had no insurance, no job, no credit, and no vehicle for a long time. I had seven children with one on the way, bills I couldn't pay, health issues, but I was learning to strengthen myself in the Lord. Since this was a period of years we are talking about, I got to hear a lot of good music and preaching. Now, I had my moments. Believe me, I had my moments, but I decided, in spite of my moments or my weaknesses, I was going to seek the Lord. Neither sin in my life nor my circumstances was going to stop me from going after the prize. You know what happened next? I started hearing that still small voice a little more and a little more. As He spoke to me, I got stronger and stronger. Until June 1, 2010, arrived and I woke up with an unexpected visitor!

As I shared earlier, the Lord showed up while I was asleep, in the early morning. I experienced what I call and believe was an encounter with Jesus—not with my natural eyes and ears, but with the eyes and ears of my spirit. After that event, I was changed forever. I received such an awakening and impartation that I felt elevated inside to a higher place. The depression was all but gone, and I began to feel a sense of purpose and destiny again—a feeling I had not felt, or wanted to feel, for years. I was going to make it, if I stuck with the plan. Since 2010, there has been a divine acceleration in my life, and I am blessed, and so glad to be a child of God. We are going to continue on this path: the path of living and moving and having our being in Him.

What I want for you to know is that God never leaves you nor forsakes you. I cannot say that God will not allow circumstances that would tempt you to believe otherwise, but He is always aligning our paths for the purpose of fulfilling our destinies. With God, all things are possible, even when it most certainly seems otherwise. God loves to prove who He is to us and His great big love for us. It is in this place where I have learned a greater measure of obedience through my sufferings. When you share in His sufferings, you belong to a great fraternity in the spirit of God.

THE WORD OF THE PRODIGAL

I am the prodigal son. I am he that turned away from my Father and hardened my heart. I am he who thought my brother was crazy to stay. I am he who left against his Father's wishes. I am also he who lost my inheritance for a bowl of soup. I am he who disappointed his friends. I am he who lived in the thorn tree. I am he who lived in a pit, who wandered in the wilderness, who was imprisoned. I am he who was forgotten. I am he who no one knows. I am he who ate the king's delicacies. I am he that lost his way, that got cut off, that would not put away childish things. I am he that unrighteously judged. I am the prodigal.

I am the one who remembered his Father's house. I am the one who wanted to be His servant. I am the one He saw from afar off, the one He ran to and embraced, the one He wept over. I am the one who told Him I had sinned against Him. I am the one who wanted only to be a good servant in His house. Yet, I am the one He put His ring on, and He covered me with His best robe. I am he my Father threw a party for.

But it was my brother who was so upset. It was my brother who stayed and worked hard in the fields. It was my brother who could not see. It was my brother who would not enter my Father's celebration for me because it was me he could not stand to see. It is my brother who thought he had earned that right. But it was my brother who was told by my Father that what He was giving me had always been my brother's to have. It was my brother who felt he had earned the ring, the robe, and the celebration. It was my brother who walked away sad…who walked away mad.

It was my Father who did these things: who longed for my return, who saw greatness in me, who never gave up. It was my Father's love and kindness that led me home. It was my Father who wept over me and restored me. It was my Father who set me apart. It was my Father who received me when no one else would. It was my Father's grace that let me in. It was my Father's joy that gave me strength. It was my Father who celebrated me. It was my Father's good pleasure to see this day, given to me.

I am the prodigal who stands unashamed. I am not ashamed of my Father. It is my Father I want to please. I am the prodigal. I am the one who carries my Father's word. I am the one He blessed. I am the one He is unashamed of. I am the one He freely gives to. I am His son. What He gave me did not come from man; it is not man's to give. What He gave me cannot be taken by man; it is not theirs to take. I am the son who has been established by his Father. I will not apologize for what my Father has done. I will not apologize for what He tells me to say. I am the prodigal who has the résumé of shame and weakness. I am the prodigal who finds my

Father's strength when I am weak. I am His favored one, the one Jesus first loved. I am the prodigal.

CHAPTER 19

Final Thoughts

In the 1930's, there was a word given to a group of men of a final revival that was coming, to which there would be no end. Arthur Burt from the United Kingdom was one of those men. During this period, Arthur Burt travelled with Smith Wigglesworth, and there was an astonishing outpouring of healing, signs, and wonders. For years he was the only one living that actually heard that word. Bob Jones was another from the United States who received this same type word, and at the time, the two had no knowledge of each other. From all accounts, Bob Jones believed he would see the beginning of this move before he died. In the late 1980s, Bob Jones felt he was supposed to encourage a man in Great Britain. Rev. Steve Scroggs, writes this account in "The Awakening of the Lord's End of Days":

One morning in the late 1980's, when Bob was praying and talking to God, the Lord told Bob that he wanted him to encourage one of his men in Great Britain. The Lord said, "In the year you were born, I gave him a word, and he has not seen this word fulfilled. Tell him that he will see this word come to pass before he dies."

The way I understand it, Bob Jones told this word to someone who had just returned from England, who had just been at this man's house, the one Bob was supposed to encourage. The person said that they had just visited Arthur Burt. From all accounts, this word Bob Jones sent meant a lot to Arthur Burt. In 2014, both Bob Jones and Arthur Burt died. Arthur Burt was 102 when he died. I was riding down the highway when I believe the Lord spoke this to my heart:

This revival with no intended end has started, yet there is a key and a warning that must be heard. The keys to this revival are the combined messages of the two prophets who carried this prophetic word. Bob Jones was asked, and he asked, "Did you learn to love?" Arthur Burt brought a deeper insight of humility. Those two men were marked by these words. My church must walk in both, with the wisdom of both revelations firmly planted. It is the combination of love and humility that will keep legs under this movement. Love and humility are defined by human standards but in reality are actually the synonymous winds that define the essence of Love Himself. These are two keys to the Kingdom that must be found. The knowledge of Kingdom keys does not equal the effective possession for their use. To turn these keys requires transformation from the wisdom of these keys. If this doesn't happen, then this generation could repeat what every generation before it has. When My Spirit moves, the mistake of the previous generation has always been entering into elitism. Elitism is neither love nor humility, and My Glory will not rest on the snobbery of men. Once the people who receive a move of My Spirit enter into elitism, they will quickly become an irrelevant wineskin of what once was that the next generation will soon scoff at. Do not scoff at the previous generations or walk pridefully in the knowledge of the things known or things to come. If you have already done this, you have already begun to step into elitism. Turn away from that heart condition, and don't be captured by it again. To eat from the Tree of Life requires the understanding of grace. A true revelation of My grace gives no man any reason to boast. Everything man has was given to Him. Therefore, seek out and ask for the wisdom of these instructions, and there will indeed be no end!

Amen.

It is important that we behold Jesus in His glory. When we see Him in His glory, we are revealed with Him in glory. We indeed become who and what we behold. It is when we see who we are in Him that enables us to be who we are in Him. Yet, it is the vision we see that can easily lead us to the place of elitism. So, it is just as important that we see our humanity at the same time. It is the paradox of these seemingly opposing realities that produce life. It is these two realities that protect us from falling off the cliff of elitism. It is the embracing of who we are in Him unashamedly, as well as judging ourselves truthfully, that expresses the person of Christ. We are the stable where revival is born. Our lives are set like flint to be presence-purposed children of God. So, here is a poem I wrote not long ago that I believe encompasses these realities:

"THE HAGGARD MAN"

There once was a young man,
He stood strong and handsome.
He seemed full of talent, but somewhat a rascal.
He thought the whole world would one day adore him,

So he took to the road that winded before him.

He thought he must find the place of his throne,

Along like the others he'd gather his own.

And gather he did with wide open doors,

Drug addicts, thieves, hustlers, and whores.

All of them used him—he used them as well,

But it finally caught up to him under a spell.

So he came to his senses; he got on his knees.

He cried out to Jesus to take him in, please.

And Jesus responded to this man's request,

He took him right in and gave him His best.

The young man was happy; he felt he was cured,

And he lived for this Jesus as best that he could.

He made proclamations of things he would do:

To live for this God who was holy and true.

He thought surely now the folks would adore him,

So he took to the road that winded before him.

He thought he must find the place of his throne,

Along like the others he'd gather his own.

And gather he did with wide open doors;

They built up his ego—they truly adored.

He tried to resist this wonderful bliss,

But found himself falling into the abyss.

It seemed that he could not find the end

Of this pit to which he had fallen in.

Finally, the end of this treacherous fall

Was just the beginning—no end at all.

A deluge of suffering, a crushing to powder,

The voices of devils, louder and louder.

They all said he's through, there's just nothing left,

Even the haggard man said it himself.

For he knew he was different; things weren't the same;

He found himself broken, abused, and ashamed.

He lost everything that he'd ever owned,

He hid in a bottle—for years this went on.

Then in the night he sensed the familiar.

He sensed an old friend who came like a pillar.

He sat up awakened, and somewhat surprised,

He knew he must listen—he knew he must rise.

The Master was calling, and He said He's not mad,

The haggard man wept, but never so glad.

He felt all the poison leaving his mind

That left him so helpless, wounded, and blind.

He felt so alive for the first time in years,

With a heart that was softened, healed through the tears.

So he started to write these things in his heart,

Always with Jesus, never to part.

And though there were pains in his body he felt,

They were simple reminders of what he was dealt.

In a life full of sorrows, heartaches, and pain,

He now found the beauty of Heaven remained.

Sometimes he still hears the voices of old

That lie to him constantly, leaving him cold.

But he keeps moving forward with his hat in his hand,

For now he knows he's a haggard man.

Being fully dependent on the grace he was given

Keeps him pressing towards the life he is living.

For it isn't by accolades, power, and might,

Just the voice of the One who gives him his sight.

He feels surely now the folks won't adore him,

So he takes to the road that's winding before him.

But unlike before when he searched for his throne,

He knows that the others to him do not belong.

Yet he opens the doors as wide as before,

In come the drug addicts, the thieves, and the whores.

And he tells them the story of the haggard man

Who fumbled his life and sunk in the sand.

Then he tells of the One who sits on the throne,

Of loving forgiveness and grace to His own.

One by one they lay down their lives

At the feet of the One who looked in their eyes.

And when they look in the eyes of the old haggard man,

They know that experience comes with a plan

Of things they too will one day endure,

Though they follow a God who is holy and sure.

Life is the process that teaches the learned,

Leaving not one pride-filled stone unturned.

So if you look and you see an old man haggard,

Walking along with a limp and a stagger,

Rejoice in the story that you've been told

Of the haggard man and his God-humbled soul.

It is the journey of life. It is my story, and it is your story that this world needs. Not a painted-up perfection absent of the bruises that come along the way, but the reality of war and peace, blood and roses, pits and platforms, tragedy yet triumph, pain yet peace, failure yet overcoming—it is the presence-purposed life in the midst of the evil wisdom of this age that confounds scholars, angers rulers, and overthrows the advances of the kingdom of darkness in this world. It is the very presence of God in and on ordinary men, women, and children that hell fears: contenders of His presence. This is who we are. This is who you are. Now the question I have to ask is this: Are you the one, or should we look for another?

MY PRAYER FOR YOU

Father, again I pray for every person who has read this book, that they know You just as You are, and that they are assured that not only do You know them, but they know and understand that You love them just as they are; that they may know the riches of Your glory; that they will experience effectively what it is to be baptized into Christ; that they may live by every word that proceeds presently from Your mouth; and that they may indeed live and move and have their being in You. I ask that You manifest Yourself to each one more profoundly than they have ever experienced. I pray that they be one with You just as Jesus prayed that You and He were one. We thank You that You have made us one with you according to the finished work of the cross. To You be the glory, forever, and ever. Amen

Coming soon, Lord willing: *The Presence-Purposed Church.*

Made in the USA
Middletown, DE
29 May 2017